A Binding Knot

Guidelines to Marriage in Islam

AF479795

TRANSCRIBED AND EDITED FROM
DR. MUHAMMAD SALAH'S LECTURE

Published by:

Unit No. E-10, 5 Jln SS 15/4G, Subang Square,
47500 Subang Jaya, Selangor, Malaysia
+603-5612-2407 (office) / +6017-399-7411 (mobile)
info@tertib.press
www.tertib.press
@tertibpress (Facebook & Instagram)

Author	:	Dr Muhammmad Salah
Transcriber & Editor	:	Norashikin Azizan
Proofreader	:	Nadiah Aslam
		Arisha Mohd Affendy
Cover designer	:	Abdul Adzim Md Daim
Typesetter	:	Abdul Adzim Md Daim

A BINDING KNOT: GUIDELINES TO MARRIAGE IN ISLAM

First Edition: May 2023

Contents

Contents iii

Foreword 1

Introduction 3

Marriage in Islam 6

Finding *sakinah*, *mawaddah* and *raḥmah* in your spouse 6

Invoking Allah (s.w.t.) to make our spouse and children
leaders of the righteous 9

Covering the imperfections of our spouse 11

Avoiding the haram by lowering our gaze 14

Love in Islam 20

The Rules of Marriage in Islam 26

Why Do We Marry? 28

Lowering your gaze 29

Guarding your chastity 34

Act of worship   37

Fulfilling half of our *deen*   39

A means of getting rich   42

Procreation   44

To raise goodly daughters   48

Legal Status of Marriage in Islam   59

Waliyy   66

Choosing the Right Spouse   74

The Pursuit   80

Istikharah   88

Engagement   97

ʿIddah   100

Nikaḥ   104

Mahr   114

Walimah   120

Q&A   124

Foreword

In a world filled with ever-changing dynamics and evolving notions of love and commitment, *A Binding Knot* arrives as a steadfast beacon, illuminating the sanctity and significance of marriage in the context of Islamic teachings. Grounded in the timeless wisdom of the Qur'an, this transcendent book serves as a guiding light for couples embarking on the sacred journey of matrimony.

In Surah an-Nisa', we encounter a profound verse that beckons us to reflect on the depth and beauty of the marriage contract—a "firm and strong covenant". It is within this divine framework that *A Binding Knot* artfully explores the multifaceted layers of love, trust, and responsibility that intertwine to create the foundation of a thriving marital union.

This meticulously transcribed and edited book serves as an invaluable resource, drawing upon the rich teachings of Islam to provide an encompassing understanding of marriage and family life. The pages within reveal an insightful exploration of the moral and ethical dimensions that underpin these sacred relationships. It is a testament to the transformative power of faith and the potential for marital harmony when aligned with the divine principles outlined in the Qur'an.

A Binding Knot skillfully interweaves practical guidance and spiritual wisdom, ensuring that readers are equipped not only with a theoretical understanding but also with tangible tools to nurture and strengthen their marital bonds. The author's compassionate voice gently accompanies couples on their journey, offering solace, encouragement, and direction, even in the face of challenges and uncertainties.

As you embark on this profound voyage through the pages of *A Binding Knot,* may you find solace in the timeless words of the Qur'an and discover the limitless potential of a harmonious and fulfilling marriage. This book stands as a testament to the transformative power of faith, reminding us that within the sacred union of marriage lies the potential for personal growth, deep connection, and the realisation of our true selves.

May your hearts be receptive, your minds be open, and your souls be enriched by the wisdom contained within these pages. Embrace the profound teachings and guidance offered by *A Binding Knot,* and may it serve as a treasured companion as you navigate the wondrous path of marital bliss.

Tertib Publishing

Introduction

As Muslims, it is important for us to equip ourselves with the knowledge of marriage in Islam. One of the main purposes of learning about the guidelines for marriage in Islam is to attain comfort and peace of mind. This is in the Qur'an. Allah (s.w.t.) linked getting married to the right spouse to attaining peace of mind, comfort and *sakinah*. So this compilation guides us to comprehend the *aḥkam* of marriage and divorce. Most of the questions received on *Ask Huda* or elsewhere are basically because people act first without knowledge and then resort to asking. For example, in the case of marriage:

"I married a non-Muslim guy. Is it halal or haram?"

Or in the case of divorce:

"I uttered 'divorce' three times. Does it count as one or three?"

"I divorced my wife four times. What am I supposed to do now?"

What we are supposed to do is to learn before we act.

This is what we are about to do *inshā'Allāh* with this book. Obviously, learning the dos and don'ts in marriage is also to become a better spouse in order to copy and follow the footsteps of the Prophet (s.a.w.) who said in a hadith:

خَيْرُكُـمْ خَيْرُكُمْ لِأَهْلِهِ وَأَنَـا خَيْرُكُـمْ لِأَهْلِـي وَإِذَا مَـاتَ صَاحِبُكُـمْ فَدَعُـوهُ

The best of you is he who is best to his family, and I am the best among you to my family. When one of you dies speak no ill of him.

Mishkat al-Maṣabiḥ 3252, 3253

He (s.a.w.) said that the best of you is the one who is good to his spouse; to his wife and indeed, I am the one who is the best to his spouse and his family. Obviously, that is the Prophet (s.a.w.). To fulfil what Allah (s.w.t.) has mentioned in *ayah* number 6 of Surah at-Taḥrim:

يَـٰٓأَيُّهَا ٱلَّذِيـنَ ءَامَنُـوا قُـوٓا أَنفُسَـكُمْ وَأَهْلِيكُـمْ نَـارًا وَقُودُهَا ٱلنَّـاسُ وَٱلْحِجَـارَةُ عَلَيْهَا مَلَـٰٓئِكَةٌ غِلَاظٌ شِـدَادٌ لَّا يَعْصُـونَ ٱللَّـهَ مَـآ أَمَرَهُـمْ وَيَفْعَلُـونَ مَـا يُؤْمَـرُونَ ﴿٦﴾

O' you who have believed, protect yourselves and your families from a Fire whose fuel is people and stones, over which are [appointed] angels, harsh and severe; they do not disobey Allah in what He commands them but do what they are commanded.

So, because of that, I perceived that this course is very crucial and of great importance and significance.

Marriage in Islam

Finding sakinah, mawaddah and raḥmah in your spouse

In Surah ar-Rum, Allah (s.w.t.) listed some of his countless blessings. This includes the creation of the heavens and the Earth, and our creation originally from *turab* (soil) and then from *nutfah* (male's sperm and female eggs). He also mentioned the alternation and the diversity of our mother tongues and ethnicities. Allah (s.w.t.) also mentioned that among His blessings and favours upon us He has created for us spouses from among ourselves—a life mate. So, He (s.w.t.) says:

وَمِنْ ءَايَـٰتِهِۦٓ أَنْ خَلَقَ لَكُم مِّنْ أَنفُسِكُمْ أَزْوَٰجًا لِّتَسْكُنُوٓا۟ إِلَيْهَا وَجَعَلَ بَيْنَكُم مَّوَدَّةً وَرَحْمَةً ۚ إِنَّ فِى ذَٰلِكَ لَآيَـٰتٍ لِّقَوْمٍ يَتَفَكَّرُونَ ﴿٢١﴾

And of His signs is that He created for you from yourselves mates that you may find tranquility in them, and He placed between you affection and mercy. Indeed in that are signs for a people who give thought.

And among His countless blessings and signs that He is the Only One who is worthy of worship—that He has created for us from among ourselves; spouses. What is the purpose? The number one objective is to find *sakinah*, which is repose, comfort, and peace of mind. In order to achieve this condition of *sakinah*, He developed and created between the spouse *mawaddah* (affection) and *raḥmah* (mercy). You will find that Allah (s.w.t.) did not mention the word 'love' or 'hope'. He mentioned what is more important, where 'love' will be included and whether it is there or not at least compassion and mercy will continue to exist in order for both couples to enjoy *sakinah*—repose, comfort and peace of mind. Indeed, in the creation of spouses and life mates for us human beings, there is a great *ayah*; a great sign but for those who ponder and reflect. I remember, when somebody comes to my house in the States, I have some *da'wah* materials to pass on to them and talk to them about Islam. So, once I had an Internet technician working in my house. So, I chatted with him to break the ice and started talking to him about Islam. I asked him whether he is married and whether he has kids. He said, "Yes, I have three kids. But I'm not married." I said, "Why not? You already have three kids with her, why aren't you married?" He said, "If I marry her, she can divorce me and take my house. And I am the one who paid for the house. I'm not giving my house to anyone." So here, he realised that the marriage relationship had turned into a battlefield. This is true in the mind of many people. Simply because you are not interested in the Divine Constitution. You do not like the Divine Guidance. You want to go your way. So, eventually, people end up deviating and living a miserable life. So even though they criticise Islam and Muslims for whatever traditions they maintain, but the highest rate of domestic violence ever is in such societies and whenever somebody gets killed—the number one suspect—is the spouse. So, if the wife is killed, the number suspect one is the husband. If the husband is killed, the number one suspect is the wife. Of course, this is the kind of life which Allah (s.w.t.) referred to and wanted us to experience when He said:

And of His signs is that He created for you from yourselves mates

Why? The answer is:

that you may find tranquility

Invoking Allah (s.w.t.) to make our spouse and children leaders of the righteous

In Surah al-Furqan, verse 63, Allah (s.w.t.) towards the end of the surah counted some of the very prominent traits of *Ibadurraḥman*. And among the traits of the servants of the Most Beneficent is this practice of making supplication a regular routine.

$$وَعِبَادُ ٱلرَّحْمَـٰنِ ٱلَّذِينَ يَمْشُونَ عَلَى ٱلْأَرْضِ هَوْنًا وَإِذَا خَاطَبَهُمُ ٱلْجَـٰهِلُونَ قَالُوا سَلَـٰمًا ﴿٦٣﴾$$

And the servants of the Most Merciful are those who walk upon the earth easily, and when the ignorant address them [harshly], they say [words of] peace,

Allah (s.w.t.) said in Surah Furqan, 74:

$$وَٱلَّذِينَ يَقُولُونَ رَبَّنَا هَبْ لَنَا مِنْ أَزْوَٰجِنَا وَذُرِّيَّـٰتِنَا قُرَّةَ أَعْيُنٍ وَٱجْعَلْنَا لِلْمُتَّقِينَ إِمَامًا ﴿٧٤﴾$$

And those who say, "Our Lord, grant us from among our wives and offspring comfort to our eyes and make us a leader [i.e., example] for the righteous."

Marriage is not only to enjoy the physical relationship and that is it. You must have deep thinking and long planning which is: Who is going to be the mother or father of your kids? Not only that, but you must also think about who is going to be the grandparents—paternal or maternal of your kids. This is important before you make the decision because marriage is not just about you, liking a girl and she likes you back, and "We have chemistry" and then you both get married. No, it is more than that. It is merging and joining two families. Not only two individuals. So, the *du'a'* of *Ibadurrahman* is for our spouses and offspring.

A man came to Iman al-Ḥasan al-Basri (r.a.h.) and said, "My wife is already pregnant, and I came to ask you about the proper way to raise my child." He (r.a.h.) said, "It's too late." The man said, "She's just pregnant." Then Imam al-Ḥasan (r.a.h.) said that he should have asked the question before he got married. Before you have made your decision about whom you are going to marry. This is important regarding the upbringing of the children and deciding the future of your offspring. Even through marriage, we ask Allah (s.w.t.) for us to be superior in *taqwa* and *iman*, not just to settle for being righteous. Rather be leaders and righteous. Leaders in righteousness and piety:

Waj'alnā lilmuttaqīna imāmā

Covering the imperfections of our spouse

There are some verses in the Qur'an tackling the concept of marriage and the binding knot. Very powerful, very eloquent and unprecedented and unmatched in any book, in any religion, in any faith or ideology. When Allah (s.w.t.) refers to marriage as *al-Mithakul Ghaliz* (the binding knot), the most powerful contract. And when Allah (s.w.t.) refers to the relationship between the husband and wife as *libas*. Do you know what *libas* is? *Libas* is the outfit. The undergarment is the closest thing to your flesh. So your spouses or your *libas*. In Surah al-Baqarah verse 187, Allah (s.w.t.) mentioned:

$$\text{...هُنَّ لِبَاسٌ لَّكُمْ وَأَنتُمْ لِبَاسٌ لَّهُنَّ}$$

Your spouses are a garment for you as you are
for them...

Hunna refers to the wives. They are your garments as you are their garments. When a child reaches the age of puberty, he or she starts having what is known as *'awrah*. Can a girl sit at home in front of her parents and siblings, wearing a pair of shorts? No, that is haram. The *'awrah* is up to the knees, right? And it is the same for the boy. But for husband and wife, there is no *'awrah*. A man can see every part of his wife, and a wife can see her husband's. There is no restriction. There is no *'awrah*. And we will find here amazing narrations of how these houses of the prophets, whether our 'A'ishah (r.a), who was the youngest, or Umm Salamah (r.a.); the oldest or Hafsah (r.a.) or Sawdah (r.a.) or others, narrating and sharing with us, even pertaining to the intimate relationship with the Prophet (s.a.w.) and performing *ghusl* in the nude. So, it is very important for us to get acquainted with all these ahadith in order to know the nature of this relationship and what is halal and what is haram in this regard.

With regards to the *ayah* which is of Surah al-Baqarah verse 187, it comes with a package of responsibilities. That means if you share anything with your spouse, no matter what is it, this is very confidential. It should not be shared with anyone else. Yes, you love your parents most, but what happened now? You have a partner, a soulmate, not just a spouse. So, he should feel very comfortable sharing with you all his secrets and vice versa. She should feel very safe to share with you everything about her personal and confidential life. And then that represents the fact that *your spouses are a garment for you as you are for them*—clothes cover not only the *'awrah* but also imperfections. Imperfections of your body, so if you see any imperfection or drawback in your spouse that should not be exposed nor revealed or shared with anyone for whatever reason, keep it. Each spouse should cover his or her spouse's false errors, and mistakes and keep their secrets especially what goes on during the intimate relationship. I attended once a conversation: A young man got married and somebody was asking him "How did it go?" And he said, "*Bismillāh*," and started narrating everything to the extent of taking off her clothes. So, I said, "Wait, wait a minute. What are you talking about?" He said he was asking what happened. No. Just say, "*Alḥamdulillāh*." You do not share the details of what happened in your bedroom. This is very confidential. You don't even share it with your own parents. Neither you nor her. Due to the following hadith, obviously, non-Muslims do, and non-practising Muslims don't mind doing it as well. Revealing these confidential facts, which go on in the bedroom during the intimate relationship; they share it with others. Sometimes to brag about it, sometimes to complain. None of that is permissible.

Abu Sa'id al-Khudri in a sound hadith collected by Muslim. He (r.a.) narrated that the Prophet (s.a.w.) said:

"Verily, the most evil of people in the presence of Allah on the Day of Resurrection is a man who was intimate with his wife and then spreads her secrets."

Ṣaḥīḥ Muslim 1437

The Prophet (s.a.w.) was the politest. So, for words pertaining to sexual activities, he would use a metaphor. Whatever goes on between you, both in the bedroom is absolutely forbidden to be shared with anyone else. Such a person is accursed by Allah (s.w.t.).

Avoiding the haram by lowering our gaze

Among the beauties and benefits of marriage is it helps to restrain the person from the haram—by lowering the gaze and dismissing any evil thoughts that may cross the person's mind, whether it's he or she. For instance, in the sound hadith which is collected by Imam Muslim:

Jabir reported that the Prophet (s.a.w.) saw a woman, and so he came to his wife, Zaynab, as she was tanning a leather and had sexual intercourse with her. He then went to his Companions and told them:

> The woman advances and retires in the shape of a devil, so when one of you sees a woman, he should come to his wife, for that will repel what he feels in his heart.

Ṣaḥīḥ Muslim 1403a

There is a huge difference between Islamic and non-Islamic etiquette and the dos and don'ts in this regard. This means that the Prophet (s.a.w.) said, if you while at work or in the seat—he is addressing men who are most likely to work and get in touch with others in the marketplace and so on. If you see the beauty of a woman, which may attract you and impress you, or arouse you, then return home and have an intimate relationship with your wife that will satisfy you and that will restrain you from thinking about the haram. What is haram? When a person thinks about a woman who is not lawful for him, this is haram. So mere thinking is not permissible.

I'd love to share with you this very inspiring statement by Ibn Qayyim. May Allah have mercy on him. He said when an evil thought pertaining to haram, a lustful desire for instance; crosses your mind, ward it off. Close the doors, say *Astaghfirullāh*. Do not allow yourself to get fascinated with it, to think about it, to daydream. Oh man, what if that is not permissible? And what if you let go and you keep thinking about it and you just keep daydreaming? Then he will turn into a contemplation, something after it was haram. Now you desire to achieve it even though you know it is haram and that happens as a result of constantly thinking about it and you do not make any effort to ward it off or to stop thinking about it. And as a result of contemplating that, unfortunately at the earliest opportunity, you may fall into sins, including adultery. So, what happens is through my experience in the field of counselling. I have even received some messages recently. Those who are involved in watching porn. After the action then he was only, you know, their desire to see sexual relation. One thing leads to another, so that have developed in them all the odd ideas. Even having sexual relations with anything. So, what we consider is taboo and LGBT and even sexual relations with animals because he watches this, and they think about it and plural sexual relations. He admits that I have become addicted to watching this, and I even think all the time about being part of that. So, after it was something that once you think about it you say *a ʿūdhubillāhiminashayṭānirrajim*, how could a normal human being or a sane *insan* think about it? Now gradually because the person allowed himself to watch it once, twice, 10, 20, 100 times. It has become the norm. So, his resistance and his immune system with regards to the haram have become very weak and that person has become very vulnerable. So, at the earliest opportunity, he or she may fall into the haram. Because there is zero immunity. There is no resistance whatsoever. They have been fantasising about what they see and once they can do it, even though they know it is a major sin, they might fall into it. May Allah protect us all.

The Prophet (s.a.w.) tells us if you see anything that you like or for instance, a woman outside, *Alḥamdulillāh*, you have your wife. Go and satisfy your desire in a lawful fashion. It will ward it off because it is all about satisfying this desire so once it is taken care of, even if a beauty queen is in front of you, she will not be tempting you anymore. In addition to remembering what Allah (s.w.t.) has mentioned twice in the Qur'an, once in Surah al-A'raf, verse 200:

$$\text{وَإِمَّا يَنزَغَنَّكَ مِنَ ٱلشَّيْطَـٰنِ نَزْغٌ فَٱسْتَعِذْ بِٱللَّهِ ۚ إِنَّهُۥ سَمِيعٌ عَلِيمٌ ۝}$$

And if an evil suggestion comes to you from Satan, then seek refuge in Allah. Indeed, He is Hearing and Knowing.

So, whenever an evil thought comes from *shayṭan* crosses your mind, what you are supposed to do is say *a'ūdhubillāhiminashshayṭānirrajim*. Seek refuge with Allah against *ash-Shayṭanirrajim*. *Innahū sami'ul'alim*—indeed Allah is All-Hearer, All-Knowing. Allah (s.w.t.) will ward off this evil thought from you. In Surah Fussilat verse 36, it has the same verse, but it ends with *innahū huwa as-sami'ul'alim:*

وَإِمَّا يَنزَغَنَّكَ مِنَ ٱلشَّيْطَٰنِ نَزْغٌ فَٱسْتَعِذْ بِٱللَّهِ ۚ إِنَّهُۥ هُوَ ٱلسَّمِيعُ ٱلْعَلِيمُ ﴿٣٦﴾

And if there comes to you from Satan an evil suggestion, then seek refuge in Allah. Indeed, He is the Hearing, the Knowing.

I am going to share with you something that I am sure all of you would like to know about. How can I differentiate between the temptation which is coming from *shaytan* versus the temptation which is coming from my inner desire? This is because it is not all *shaytan*. For instance, Ramadan is just around the corner. Does it mean since all the *shaytan* are being chained, we are not committing sins anymore? And those who do bad will not do bad anymore? No! Some people will continue doing what is haram, even major sins. They indulge in major sins even during Ramadan, even during *Laylatul Qadr*. That is because it is not only about *shaytan*. There is the inner desire. How to distinguish between a sin or a desire, or an urge to commit a sin because of the temptation of *shaytan* or because of the inner desire? Simple. *Subḥānallāh*, if it is really a matter of *shaytan*, it is very easy and affordable. If you say *aʿūdhubillāhiminashshayṭānirrajim*, *shaytan* will leave you alone. But if it is your inner desire, then it takes a lot more than that. It takes a lot of practice. It takes exercising, and resisting the haram; it takes increasing the level of your *iman* in order to be immune enough. But a person who is watching the haram or doing the haram on a regular basis, no matter how many times he says, *a'ūdhubillāhiminashshayṭānirrajīm*, *shayṭan* has nothing to do with it. You, your inner desire are worse than *shayṭan* himself.

Love in Islam

Love. Is there such a thing in Islam that is called love? Of course. As a father. As a parent. If your child comes home, a child, even if he or she is 20, will always remain a child. We will still call them kids in our eyes, even after they get married. So, for example, one day, your son, or your daughter is a college student. They share with you because they trust you: "I love this person." He or she might be their classmate, co-worker, teacher, student, patient, or doctor. "I feel like I'm in love. Is it haram? Does Islam recognise that? Is it something that we should deal with or bury it?"

Love in Islam is one of the most beautiful things. And Islam acknowledges love. Reveals it and appreciates it. Even love between a man and a woman. As long as you behave towards it in a halal fashion. When 'Amr ibn 'As (r.a.) was chosen by the Prophet (s.a.w.) as commander-in-chief in one of the expeditions and he achieved victory. When he returned victorious from the battle which is *Dhat as-Salasil*, he wanted to earn a title and honour from the Prophet (s.a.w.). So, he asked him a question. He said, "O' Rasulullah. Whom do you love most?" And he was expecting the Prophet (s.a.w.) at this particular moment to say, "You." because he achieved victory. "Whom do you love most?" And the Prophet (s.a.w.) without thinking, said "'A'ishah." He said, "No, no, no, I don't mean woman." He (s.a.w.) said, "Her father. If not 'A'ishah, then her father." And he asked, "Who next?" The Prophet (s.a.w.) said: "'Umar." (From Ṣaḥīḥ Muslim 2384).

So, the catch in this hadith is that the Prophet (s.a.w.) did not hesitate to reveal his love to 'A'ishah (r.a.) to the public. It is perfectly OK to say, "I love my wife" and for the wife to say, "I love my husband" and it would be best if they both can frequently exchange these words to express the feeling that they truly love each other. So, love is appreciated. Love is a great thing, but sometimes it is very painful. And sometimes it is haram—when a man falls in love with a woman whom he knows that she is not available. She is married, for example. So you know, you don't say, "I love her." This is an evil thought. This is what you need to say *a'ūdhubillāhiminashshaytānirrajim*. Maybe the woman is engaged or maybe she is our maḥram. That is not permissible. And also when a person knows that he or she is not in a position of marrying this person. For whatever reason it is not feasible; it is not going to happen. Then you should overcome this love and try your best to overcome it and forgive it and bury it even though it is not easy. There will be a bunch of ahadith in this regard. But halal is halal and haram is haram. Look at this instance. The Prophet (s.a.w.) spoke about love—when a man loves a woman, or when a woman loves a man, and whenever too, a man and a woman are in love. So he acknowledged that and he said here is a solution. If you are in love and there is chemistry between you, then get married. But sometimes the obstacle is the parents. Whether the guardian of the girl. Whether the mother of the boy is not from our class, from our type, from our ethnicity or whatever, then you will find the (s.w.t.) Allah himself intervened in the Qur'an to command the *waliyy* not to be an obstacle as long as both are righteous. The guy is capable to take care of the wife, to provide a house, to support the wife and the family, and he is a practising Muslim. Then you should facilitate this relationship in a legal way, said in the Ṣaḥīḥ hadith which is collected by Imam Muslim.

There is no other solution for those who are in love other than getting married. If you are in love, think about it. You love your classmate. Or is this what you think? In the States, whenever we have summer camps, on the second or third day, immediately every boy and girl becomes boyfriends and girlfriends. And based on that, this relationship permits them even to sleep together. So I got hold of two—whom I was supervising, a boy and a girl. I just asked them. "You just met a couple of days ago, on what basis you decided to become her boyfriend and on what basis you chose him to be your boyfriend?" So it was all superficial as a result of watching too many movies. He says, "She cares a lot about me." I asked further to the girl. "What made you think that he would be the best partner?" She said, "Well, he's cool." Being cool does not establish a house; does not support a wife, does not guarantee supporting a family and children and all of that. But you see them at night together. So this relationship may result in a child who will be born out of wedlock from an Islamic perspective and the worst part is they do not mind. And that is why they only teach them to have safe sex. You can have sex as much as you want as long as you avoid getting pregnant. *Subḥānallāh*, at a school across from my house, it is a middle school. In that school, they have babysitting facilities. Do you know why? This is because the girls—in their 11th and 12th grades—not only that they are pregnant, but they come to school with their babies. They got impregnated in school. *Subḥānallāh*, out of wedlock, of course. Human beings intervened and they put laws and restrictions. A 'marriageable' age is 18. This means that you are not allowed to marry before 18. But looking at the reality, you are allowed to have sex as early as the age of nine. The Prophet (s.a.w.) presented the solution. If two are in love and they can afford to get married, and the man can afford to take care of a family to support a wife. In other words, he is not a child. Then the solution is *nikah*. And as we are going to learn, *inshā'Allāh*, the word, *nikah* implies two things. The marriage contract and the sexual relations, or the consummation of the marriage. So love, including love at first sight is not something haram. Because you cannot control it. Ask anyone who is in love. How did you love her? How did you love him? What made you fall in love with him? Say once I saw him, I fell in love with him. That happens. Because there is not only chemistry but also some sort of attraction. It is out of your control. But as long as it is not based on appearance or wearing revealing clothes or sexual desire only because of all of that, it is not called love. Rather that is called sexual desire. Keep this in mind. A person who is not really educated Islamically in this regard may fall into a big trap. For instance, the Prophet (s.a.w.) said,

Narrated Abu Darda':

The Prophet (s.a.w.) said: Your love for a thing causes blindness and deafness.

Sunan Abi Dawud 5130

When a girl holds a love for someone who is not worth it, but somehow, she fell in love with him. So she consulted her parents, her friends, her teachers, and even the shaykh.

But everyone was telling her, "No, no, no, he's not the right person. Trust me." So there is a general consensus. He is not the right person, but she says, "I'm in love!" so she disregards all the views and recommendations, and she still goes with her—*not love*—but desire. Including when a girl falls in love with a non-Muslim guy. And then, even though she knows it is haram. So, she keeps calling the program that I am in and asked and shared: "But *Wallāhi*, this guy has manners better than Muslims. If he does not say *Lā ilāha ilallāh Muḥammadar Rasulullāh*, it is not permissible to marry him under any circumstances. "Well, he believes in one God." Does he believe in Rasulullah (s.a.w.) as the Messenger of Allah? "Not yet, but. I will make him." That happens all the time. And as a result, disasters take place. Girls still go forward, and they marry without the consent of their guardians, and they marry a non-Muslim guy and as a result of that, this relationship is not marriage. This relationship is pure fornication. And if the girl dismisses the *ḥukm* of Allah which does not permit a Muslim girl to marry any non-Muslim, then she might even come out of the fold of Islam. And I know some people have been in this relationship for more than twenty years. Living in pain, sorrow, and grief. But she regrets it. And she says, "What can I do? I've made the mistake and now we have kids."

There are certain procedures which *inshā'Allāh* during this course we are going to learn about them. If you really want to acquire and achieve what we mention in verse 21 of Surah ar-Rum: So that you might find repose, *sakinah*—comfort, peace of mind in them. And if you don't, there will not be any *sakinah* whatsoever. It might actually turn into a war zone. May Allah (s.w.t.) protect us against that. With regard to the same hadith, sometimes a person falls in love with a girl. Everybody says that she has an illicit relationship. She is known by that, but because he is in love with her, so he dismisses all the advice. No. You need to put forward number one: *istikharah* and along with it *istisharah*. This is because we are talking about sowing the seed in order to produce something that will benefit this *dunya* and in the hereafter.

The Rules of Marriage in Islam

So why do we need to know the *aḥkam* or the rules, the dos and do not dos of marriage and divorce not only marriage?

Firstly, it is an individual duty, not only a communal duty, it is an individual duty which *fard ayn* to all Muslims; to follow the Islamic laws, not only in matters of *ṣalah* and *zakah* and *ḥajj*. But also in and most importantly, the relationship.

Zawaj, marriage, *ṭalaq*, divorce as well as the upbringing of the children. Islam has well-defined rules about *nikaḥ* and sexual relations. What are halal and haram in this regard and how we should do it? Islam has prescribed the rules. So if you want to be a practising Muslim, then you must know the *aḥkam* in order to follow them. Not do first without knowledge then you ask. Not act, then find out about the solution in order to rectify what somebody has done wrong.

Why Do We Marry?

After all of those discussions about marriage and spouses in Islam, do you ever wonder what is the purpose of getting married anyway? I mean, besides fulfilling the sexual desire, besides meeting your life mate—a person whom you feel like you are in love with him or you are in love with her. Not everyone actually marries because he is in love or she is in love including in the West. That is why there are many matrimonial websites and matchmaking websites. You know they criticise arranged marriages in Muslim societies, but they do it every day. So sometimes you have never met this person in person, but you read the profile. Then you develop an interest and when you meet the person and you speak to him or you speak to her, you feel like you know you have a lot of things in common. So another meeting—the third one, then you decide. "Well, I think we should get married." This is obviously from an Islamic point of view.

Lowering your gaze

'Abdullah ibn Mas'ud (r.a.) said that the Prophet (s.a.w.) once addressed the saying:

> It was narrated that 'Abdullah said: "The Messenger of Allah said to us: 'O' young men, whoever among you can afford it, let him get married,'" and he quoted the same hadith.

> *Sunan an-Nasa'i 3210*

The Messenger (s.a.w.) addressed: O' young people, whoever affords to get married you should get married. He highly recommends getting married even if you are not interested. Why? Because it is better with regards to number one: lower your gaze. An ordinary human being will find an attraction to the opposite gender. I am talking about normal people, healthy people. Allah (s.w.t.) created us this way. It is not only human beings, I mean *kulli shay'in halaqna zawjaini ithnain.* Everything is created in pairs. Even the electrons, even the bacteria, gram-positive and gram-negative. Even in the case of the virus. So being attracted to the opposite gender—this is a very normal feeling. In order to do it in a halal way, get married and if you get married, it will help you lower your gaze. As a result of lowering your gaze, it will guide you to guard your chastity. In Surah an-Nur, there are two consecutive verses, 30 and 31. Allah (s.w.t.) commends the believers. First, the believing men and in the following are the believing women, He (s.w.t.) says:

قُل لِّلْمُؤْمِنِينَ يَغُضُّوا مِنْ أَبْصَـٰرِهِمْ وَيَحْفَظُوا فُرُوجَهُمْ ۚ ذَٰلِكَ أَزْكَىٰ لَهُمْ ۗ إِنَّ ٱللَّهَ خَبِيرٌۢ بِمَا يَصْنَعُونَ ﴿٣٠﴾

Tell the believing men to reduce [some] of their vision and guard their private parts. That is purer for them. Indeed, Allah is [fully] Aware of what they do.

وَقُل لِّلْمُؤْمِنَٰتِ يَغْضُضْنَ مِنْ أَبْصَٰرِهِنَّ وَيَحْفَظْنَ فُرُوجَهُنَّ وَلَا يُبْدِينَ زِينَتَهُنَّ إِلَّا مَا ظَهَرَ مِنْهَا وَلْيَضْرِبْنَ بِخُمُرِهِنَّ عَلَىٰ جُيُوبِهِنَّ وَلَا يُبْدِينَ زِينَتَهُنَّ إِلَّا لِبُعُولَتِهِنَّ أَوْ ءَابَآئِهِنَّ أَوْ ءَابَآءِ بُعُولَتِهِنَّ أَوْ أَبْنَآئِهِنَّ أَوْ أَبْنَآءِ بُعُولَتِهِنَّ أَوْ إِخْوَٰنِهِنَّ أَوْ بَنِىٓ إِخْوَٰنِهِنَّ أَوْ بَنِىٓ أَخَوَٰتِهِنَّ أَوْ نِسَآئِهِنَّ أَوْ مَا مَلَكَتْ أَيْمَٰنُهُنَّ أَوِ ٱلتَّٰبِعِينَ غَيْرِ أُو۟لِى ٱلْإِرْبَةِ مِنَ ٱلرِّجَالِ أَوِ ٱلطِّفْلِ ٱلَّذِينَ لَمْ يَظْهَرُوا۟ عَلَىٰ عَوْرَٰتِ ٱلنِّسَآءِ وَلَا يَضْرِبْنَ بِأَرْجُلِهِنَّ لِيُعْلَمَ مَا يُخْفِينَ مِن زِينَتِهِنَّ وَتُوبُوٓا۟ إِلَى ٱللَّهِ جَمِيعًا أَيُّهَ ٱلْمُؤْمِنُونَ لَعَلَّكُمْ تُفْلِحُونَ ﴿٣١﴾

And tell the believing women to reduce [some] of their vision and guard their private parts and not expose their adornment except that which [necessarily] appears thereof and to wrap [a portion of] their headcovers over their chests and not expose their adornment [i.e., beauty] except to their husbands, their fathers, their husbands' fathers, their sons, their husbands' sons, their brothers, their brothers' sons, their sisters' sons, their women, that

which their right hands possess [i.e., slaves], or those male attendants having no physical desire, or children who are not yet aware of the private aspects of women. And let them not stamp their feet to make known what they conceal of their adornment. And turn to Allah in repentance, all of you, O' believers, that you might succeed.

Have you heard this before?

I know you all have heard this so many times and you know it is about lowering the gaze. And not looking at what Allah (s.w.t.) has forbidden, but there is something more than one thing in this verse. Firstly, He did not say to tell the believing men to lower their gaze completely, or otherwise, I would have to keep walking without looking up. *Lower your gaze* does not mean *you should never look up*. He didn't say that. Now he wants you to look at your loved one. Enjoy looking at her, admiring her. You have the best eyes in the world. Look at this. Look at that. And this is looking halal. OK, looking at your *maḥarim*, it is halal. So he says:

Tell the believing men to reduce [some] of their vision

Min—that is a proposition, which means to lower *some* of the gaze, not all of it. Some also refer to whenever this is something that they are not supposed to look at. Prophet Muhammad's cousin was riding on the same camel with him and a woman came to ask him, and she was not wearing a face veil in the Haram, and she had a beautiful face. So he kept staring at her and the Prophet (s.a.w.) is pushing his face in the other direction. She was not lawful for him to look at her like that. To lower **some** of their gaze. And then he said, "And guard their chastity *wallāhi.*" There is no way that one can guard his or her chastity without lowering their gaze. As a result of the emails and messages I keep receiving, when the person allows himself or herself to keep on watching, eventually he commits the act of *zina*. So in order to avoid falling into the act of *zina*, lower your gaze. So that is the right order. You will find zero resistance. You are very strong. You will realise this is a major sin. And you will be like Yusuf (a.s.), saying:

مَعَاذَ ٱللَّهِ إِنَّهُ رَبِّى أَحْسَنَ مَثْوَاىَ

[I seek] the refuge of Allah. Indeed, he is my master, who has made good my residence.

Excerpt from Surah Yusuf verse 23

So tell the believing men to lower some of their gaze in order to be capable to guard their chastity. Look at the following verse which addresses the believing women to do the same. Wait a minute. I thought lowering the gaze is only incumbent on men because women are beautiful? But it also goes the other way around. Allah (s.w.t.) also commanded the believing women to lower their gaze. Is looking at my face haram? But when does it become haram? When you like a person, and you enjoy looking at him on the screen. When he is on television, whenever he is on YouTube. And she finds a different feeling. Then she has to lower her gaze. Even though the face is not *'awrah*, to protect your chastity, ward off the evil thought before you start contemplating it. And ward it off before it turns into action. And you ward it off, even if you have done it before, it turns into a habit, an evil habit.

Guarding your chastity

Marriage will definitely, most definitely help the couple to lower their gaze in order to achieve the chastity which Allah (s.w.t.) said:

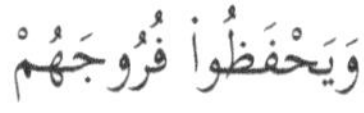

وَيَحْفَظُوا۟ فُرُوجَهُمْ

guard their private parts

Excerpt from Surah an-Nur verse 30

Al-furuj is the plural of *farj*. It is a polite word that Allah (s.w.t.) chose in the Qur'an to refer to the private part of both men and women. So the private part of a man is called *farj*. Medically, it has another meaning. And anatomically it has another name. But when you say *farj*, you can say which *farj* because it refers to masculine and feminine. The man's private part and the woman's private part. *Furujahum*—in order to guard your private parts from falling into the haram, you need to lower your gaze. And what will help you most to lower your gaze is when you are capable to satisfy this natural sexual desire in a halal fashion. I may give you an example and I hope you don't take me wrong. Somebody was fasting. And I say always avoid going shopping—food shopping whenever you are fasting because you will simply collect everything on the shelves. Everything you see, even bread. Oh, man, I want this. I love this. I love tuna fish. I love it. And you keep buying things which you are not going to eat because you are fasting. You are hungry. If you want to go shopping and take your wife shopping after you have lunch already. What happens when a person is starving? Anything he sees, he wants it so he keeps looking at this woman and at that woman, young or old, married or single, it does not matter. When a person is fully satisfied with halal as the Prophet (s.a.w.) said: Go back to your wife and enjoy an intimate relationship with her—it is like a person who happened to have a meal and then if you put a rooster or a turkey in front of him—he would say: "I'm full. I don't have room for it, *Alḥamdulillāh*, I'm satisfied." So one of the greatest means of overcoming the sexual desire towards what is haram is getting married. So what about a young man or a young woman who cannot afford to get married yet, especially nowadays, our education, you have to finish your school first. By the way, I advise parents, I tell my children at any age *Alḥamdulillāh* if you are interested and I can afford it, I will be more than happy to help you even support you financially until you are capable to stand on foot. This is because whenever you have the urge and it is a must, you do not keep forcing your child to go another three or four or five years—"No marriage before you finish your masters." Some parents are like that. "You have to finish your PhD first!" Then the girl is already 45 then you start looking. "Shaykh, can you help us to find a suitor for our daughter?" While the suitor wants 20 not 45. And there is nothing wrong with marrying at 45 or 50, but I am talking about what people are looking for normally. So if there is an urge, and if there is a need, Allah (s.w.t.) ordered the guardians to facilitate that and to help, and this is one of the greatest means of spending money. So whoever can afford to get married, let him or her get married to restrain eyes from casting evil glances and preserves one from *fahishah* (immorality).

Act of worship

What if one cannot afford it? Fasting is one way if one cannot afford marriage hadith. So why did the Prophet (s.a.w.) prescribe fasting now? It would be voluntary fasting, not only during Ramadan for a person whom he or she had this sexual desire, but they cannot afford to get married because supposedly during fasting the person will abstain from the haram and will lower their gaze. But what is happening that some people? It would not make any difference between them, even if it is Ramadan. And obviously, Islam perceives marriage as one of the great acts of worship. *Acts of worship*, yeah. Yes indeed, how?

I am sure you are all familiar with the story of the three companions who wanted to be with the Prophet (s.a.w.) in *Jannah*. In *al-Firdawsi A'la*. So they said: There is no way that we can be with him in *Jannah* unless we know what he does in private. So they visited some of the mothers of the believers and they inquired about the 'ibadah of the Prophet (s.a.w.) in private. Then each one of them came up with his own custom 'ibadah. Assuming that with good faith and intention, if I do this, Allah will love me and will bring me close to the Prophet (s.a.w.) in *Jannah*. So one of them vowed that he shall fast every single day, not only Mondays and Thursdays but every single day. And the second vowed not

to sleep at night. Why? No, he is not watching haram. He is not wasting time on social media. But he is praying from *Isha'* till *Fajr* every single night—he is doing *qiyamullayl*. And the third one vowed he will never get married. Why? He does not want anything to distract him from the *'ibadah*. This is because they might eventually have children, and no, he wants to devote himself and his life to the worship of Allah (s.w.t.). The news reached the Prophet (s.a.w.). So he gathered the entire Muslim community. And he (s.a.w.) addressed them, saying, "I am indeed the Messenger of Allah. I am the most beloved of Him and the most God-fearing. Yet, I do not fast every single day. I fast some days and I skip other days. I take a break. And I do not pray for the entire night on every single night I sleep and I rest. Then I get up to pray and I sleep again. And I'm already married. Whoever shows no interest in my tradition, he or she does not belong to me. So, if a person thinks: 'I'm not getting married because I want to devote my life to the worship of Allah (s.w.t.)', you're missing the point. Marriage itself has a variety of worship that cannot be observed unless you are married." (From Ṣaḥiḥ al-Bukhari 5063)

Fulfilling half of our deen

We are going to learn shortly that marriage undergoes the five legal *aḥkam*. But before that, do you know that marriage represents 50% of the religious commitment? In Egypt, for instance, or in the Arabic world, when a person wants to marry and they visit the girl's house or the guardian, they use a metaphor. So he says to his future father-in-law while he is proposing to marry his daughter, he said, "Uncle, I'm really interested to fulfil half of my *deen*." This is the phrase that is normally used. The Prophet (s.a.w.) said in one hadith. This hadith is very important. "When approaching your Ramadan," he said. "Whoever secures two things for me, I stand surety for him or her to enter *Jannah*." Only two things so that is easy. You wish. What is the first? What is between the jaws? What is in your mouth? *The tongue.* If you promise to control your tongue, that is number one and what is number two? What is between the thighs which is the *farj*? The private part. What does it mean to protect the private part? It is to protect yourself from falling into illicit relations. Or even the introductions which may lead to it. So the Prophet (s.a.w.) said whoever secures these two things for me, I stand surety for him or her to enter *Jannah*. (From Ṣaḥiḥ al-Bukhari 6109)

What causes people to enter Hellfire mostly is the harvest

of what they say. And the person may be praying *taḥajjud*. The person may be praying on a regular basis, but when it comes to sexual desire, he is very weak and vulnerable. So that is why the Prophet (s.a.w.) says these two things, if you control and protect them from falling into the haram or using them into what is forbidden, I promise you and I stand surety for you that you shall enter *Jannah*. When a man got married at the time of the Prophet (s.a.w.), Anas reported the Prophet (s.a.w.) as saying,

> "When a man marries he has fulfilled half of the religion; so let him fear God regarding the remaining half."
>
> Mishkat al-Maṣabiḥ 3096

What is the remaining half? The prayers, the fasting, the *zakah*, reading Qur'an, all these *'ibadah* are only fifty-percent, and marriage represents fifty-percent, yes indeed. This is because if the person is settled in this regard and does not think about the haram relationship, he or she is protected against a great deal of evil.

When you get married, it saves you from falling into sinful acts, and illicit relations. It helps you to lower your gaze, in order to avoid falling into the haram. It gives you a companion. So that you are not alone or lonely. Most of the illicit relations happen due to living alone or being alone. Do you know that the Prophet (s.a.w.) forbade living by yourself? Especially when you know that you are a victim of the *shaytan* every time you close the door behind you—you start watching what is haram, communicating in haram. And that would lead to what we mentioned earlier. It is very slippery and the steep is very sharp. So when you have a partner, especially a good partner and *Alhamdulillāh*, the chances are slim or even do not exist of falling into the haram. Now we know the origin of the saying, "I want to complete or fulfil half of my religion." and where it comes from.

A means of getting rich

وَلْيَسْتَعْفِفِ ٱلَّذِينَ لَا يَجِدُونَ نِكَاحًا حَتَّىٰ يُغْنِيَهُمُ ٱللَّهُ مِن فَضْلِهِۦ ۗ وَٱلَّذِينَ يَبْتَغُونَ ٱلْكِتَـٰبَ مِمَّا مَلَكَتْ أَيْمَـٰنُكُمْ فَكَاتِبُوهُمْ إِنْ عَلِمْتُمْ فِيهِمْ خَيْرًا ۖ وَءَاتُوهُم مِّن مَّالِ ٱللَّهِ ٱلَّذِىٓ ءَاتَىٰكُمْ ۚ وَلَا تُكْرِهُوا۟ فَتَيَـٰتِكُمْ عَلَى ٱلْبِغَآءِ إِنْ أَرَدْنَ تَحَصُّنًا لِّتَبْتَغُوا۟ عَرَضَ ٱلْحَيَوٰةِ ٱلدُّنْيَا ۚ وَمَن يُكْرِههُّنَّ فَإِنَّ ٱللَّهَ مِنۢ بَعْدِ إِكْرَٰهِهِنَّ غَفُورٌ رَّحِيمٌ ۝

But let them who find not [the means for] marriage abstain [from sexual relations] until Allah enriches them from His bounty. And those who seek a contract [for eventual emancipation] from among whom your right hands possess - then make a contract with them if you know there is within them goodness and give them from the wealth of Allah which He has given you. And do not compel your slave girls to prostitution, if they desire chastity, to seek [thereby] the temporary interests of worldly life. And if someone should compel them, then indeed, Allah is [to them], after their compulsion, Forgiving and Merciful.

Allah (s.w.t.) in Surah an-Nur verse 33 commanded the believing men and women who cannot afford the means to get married, to be patient, through observing fasting, not being alone, lowering their gaze, and it requires a great deal of patience. Allah (s.w.t.) said: Let those who cannot afford the means of marriage abstain from what is forbidden till Allah enriches them out of His bounty. And I have something to share with you. It is such great, glad tidings and good news which is: Do you know that marriage is one of the greatest means of getting rich? Not only a means to find a job and to have some sort of income, no! It is about getting rich. The Prophet (s.a.w.) said that there are three types of people whom Allah (s.w.t.) vows to assist financially; physically, and by every means, one of whom is *mujahid*, because he is doing *jihad fisabilillah* on the battlefield. So Allah will take care of his family and children in his absence. This young man is working hard in order to be capable to get married. "Because I don't want to fall into illicit relations—in haram. I want to do it in halal." So even though he's living hand-to-mouth, once he and she get married, Allah (s.w.t.) will enrich them out of His bounty; will make them not just self-sufficient, but will enrich in them, if that was their intention.

Procreation

Another reason why we get married is procreation. As a human being, our lifespan is very short, 60 to 70 years. Very few people make it to 80. And most of the lifespan is wasted between eating and drinking, working, earning your living and answering to the code of nature. 15 years under puberty. So what is left for you to fulfil the purpose for which you have created—10 years? That is not much. But heritage is what the person leaves behind. Once a person enters his or her grave, they are not earning good deeds anymore. I used to pray. But when I died, I'm not praying anymore. I used to fast. I cannot fast anymore. So where will I get the reward after death and after burial? The Prophet (s.a.w.) said that there are three ways through which he can continue earning their worth, one of which is having a righteous child. "We'll pray for you." Praying for you does not necessarily means raising the hand and invoking Allah, "O'Allah, have mercy on my father. O'Allah, bless my mother, make their graves gardens of paradise." All of that is true and included. For example, my son. I made him memorise the Qur'an. He is a doctor. He is an MD and *Mashā'Allāh* . He recites the Qur'an with a melodious voice. Somebody else did not care the least about the prayers or about the hijab, or about the only cared about: "I want my son to be an MD or a lawyer or a dentist". He achieved that. The segment, which will secure a continuation for your work, is what is related to the relationship between the servant and Allah (s.w.t.). Every time my son will be reading Qur'an, he is earning good deeds. Simultaneously, I am earning similar good deeds. Same exact word. Because of me, my son or my daughter are doing these good deeds. They go for *ḥajj*, they go for *'umrah*. They give *da'wah*. They give benefits to people. *Alḥamdulillāh*, I am earning a similar reward because that is my investment. In addition, the Prophet (s.a.w.) said in a sound hadith: A person will be in his or her grave. Then in the grave, the soul will be in *Jannah*. If the person was the believer. And then the person will experience promotion, will see his soul being promoted to a higher rank in *Jannah*. You will ask Allah: "O' Allah, what for? I mean, I have not been working. I'm retired. Why is my soul being promoted in *Jannah*? So Allah (s.w.t.) will tell him: "Your child was performing *'umrah*, and said, "O' Allah, forgive my parents, have mercy on them. Put them into the highest place in *Jannah.*" So Allah answers his *du'a'*. If you did not invest in your life towards that, where will you find somebody who will pray for you or benefit you after your death? So it is not only to maintain the family's name or to keep running the business after you take off and you leave—these are all worldly means and needs. And the biggest concern is what will benefit you when you enter the grave. Then they bury you and no one will ask about you except your own investment. Those whom you thought the *deen*, the prayers, the fasting, the *taʿah*, to give *daʿwah*, to spend on *fisabilillah*. So they are following in your footsteps. There is a true continuation of you. And *Subḥānallāh*, because you raised them properly, they also taught their children the same way. So they will be rewarded and you will receive a similar reward, not only for raising them and for what they do—but also for what your great-grandchildren are doing because you are the one who planted the seed. Having said so, when you call during the program and ask me or even in a private consultation. You say, "Shaykh, I'm doing my Masters in the UK. And I met this girl, she's not Muslim. She's a Christian. But she's a Church-going girl. And I'm interested in marrying her." So I tell you, "No, don't." You say, "Why? Is it haram?" Allah (s.w.t.) says in the Qur'an in Surah al-Maidah verse 5:

ٱلۡیَوۡمَ أُحِلَّ لَكُمُ ٱلطَّیِّبَـٰتُ ۖ وَطَعَامُ ٱلَّذِینَ أُوتُوا۟ ٱلۡكِتَـٰبَ حِلٌّ لَّكُمۡ وَطَعَامُكُمۡ حِلٌّ لَّهُمۡ ۖ وَٱلۡمُحۡصَنَـٰتُ مِنَ ٱلۡمُؤۡمِنَـٰتِ وَٱلۡمُحۡصَنَـٰتُ مِنَ ٱلَّذِینَ أُوتُوا۟ ٱلۡكِتَـٰبَ مِن قَبۡلِكُمۡ إِذَاۤ ءَاتَیۡتُمُوهُنَّ أُجُورَهُنَّ مُحۡصِنِینَ غَیۡرَ مُسَـٰفِحِینَ وَلَا مُتَّخِذِیۤ أَخۡدَانٍ ۗ وَمَن یَكۡفُرۡ بِٱلۡإِیمَـٰنِ فَقَدۡ حَبِطَ عَمَلُهُۥ وَهُوَ فِی ٱلۡءَاخِرَةِ مِنَ ٱلۡخَـٰسِرِینَ ۝

This day [all] good foods have been made lawful, and the food of those who were given the Scripture is lawful for you and your food is lawful for them. And [lawful in marriage are] chaste women from among the believers and chaste women from among those who were given the Scripture before you, when you have given them their due compensation, desiring chastity, not unlawful sexual intercourse or taking [secret] lovers. And whoever denies the faith - his work has become worthless, and he, in the Hereafter, will be among the losers.

True, it is permissible to marry a chaste Muslim woman, a chaste Christian woman, or a chaste Jewish woman. But the consequences of that, how many marriages like that lasted?

Very few. The vast majority is that they end very soon. And unfortunately, after having a child or children. Whenever I am teaching at the university, I meet college students. I recognise them by the name that they are Muslims. But then I find out that they are not Muslims. She says, "My name is Nadiah." I say it sounds like an Arabic name. She says. "Yes. My father is Egyptian." And what about your mother? "They are separated." And what about you? She said, "I followed my mother's faith." So your own child from your own line has become a *kafir*. And you know beforehand, the chances of leaving behind a kafir child are so huge. But because you are very selfish and your ambitions were very limited. You were only looking at the beauty and the love. We remember the hadith: "Whenever you are in love, it makes you blind and makes you deaf." You're not listening to anyone's advice. So we marry in order to continue our heritage, to continue earning rewards.

To raise goodly daughters

The Prophet (s.a.w.) said in the sound hadith:

> He, who brought up two girls properly till they grew up, he and I would come (together) (very closely) on the Day of Resurrection, and he interlaced

his fingers (for explaining the point of nearness between him and that person).

Ṣaḥiḥ Muslim 2631

Join my club. I have two daughters. So the Prophet (s.a.w.) delivers glad tidings and good news to parents who happen to have two daughters and treat them kindly. You raise them properly, teach them the *deen*. You make them modest until they grow up. The Prophet (s.a.w.) said in another hadith:

Whoever has three daughters and is patient towards them, and feeds them, gives them to drink, and clothes them from his wealth; they will be a shield for him from the Fire on the Day of Resurrection. If you have daughters, treating them properly and raising them correctly will protect you against Hellfire. You might wonder, doesn't this apply to boys as well? The Prophet (s.a.w.) was raised in a society that is very racist, sexist, and prejudiced. They hated girls. They love boys to the extent that if a wife happened to give birth and it is a girl, they will take her right away and slip away, dig a hole and bury her alive. They were ashamed of having girls. The Prophet (s.a.w.) is telling them, you have no idea what reward waits for you if you happen to have two daughters, take care of them, educate them until they grow up. You provide for them, you clothe them, and you teach them. They will be not only a veil for you against Hellfire, just like in this hadith, he said. They will be with me in *Jannah* like these two fingers attached to each other. Do you want to be with the Prophet (s.a.w.) in the *Firdawsi A'la?* Obviously! As a result of that, I was hoping and praying to have as many girls as possible, so our first child—I call my wife Ummu Ruqayyah—because we both wanted to have a Ruqayyah. But it happened to be a boy, OK, 'Abdul Rahman. The second time we were hoping for Ruqayyah, but it was 'Abdullah. The third might be Ruqayyah. It was Anas. Fourth was Muadh. Not Ruqayyah. And so on. You know, Allah (s.w.t.) is telling us it is all a blessing, boys or girls, and if you are blessed with girls, there is even more blessing. They will protect you against falling into the Hellfire. But remember not just simply for having girls, but for taking good care of them. And among taking good care of them is actually working hard to find a good suitor for them. In the Muslim culture in general, the suitor has to come and beg the guardian to marry his daughter. This is wrong. I'm saying it in public, if I happen to see any of my students who is really deserving, I will be the one who would approach him and say, "I have a beautiful daughter and I would like for you to marry her." I would even assist them financially. No problem whatsoever. This is among taking care of your daughters. Not to be an obstacle whenever a good person proposes to her and you say no because "I want my nephew to marry her." Do not abuse nor misuse the guardianship that Allah (s.w.t.) gave you because it is not up to you to tell her whom to marry as long as she is not making something haram or making a choice which is forbidden. So this hadith is such glad tidings. I would only marry for this reason, but this is just one of the many reasons that we have been discussing.

There is an *ayah* in the Qur'an in Surah al-Baqarah. I am sure you all know it.

$$وَمِنْهُم مَّن يَقُولُ رَبَّنَا ءَاتِنَا فِى ٱلدُّنْيَا حَسَنَةً وَفِى ٱلْءَاخِرَةِ حَسَنَةً وَقِنَا عَذَابَ ٱلنَّارِ ﴿٢٠١﴾$$

But among them is he who says, "Our Lord, give us in this world [that which is] good and in the Hereafter [that which is] good and protect us from the punishment of the Fire."

One of the greatest *tabi'in* and scholars is Sa'id ibn Musayyib (r.a.h.). *Subḥānallāh*. The Khalifah wanted to give his son in marriage or his daughter in marriage to his son. But Sa'id ibn Musayyib refused. And he looked at one of his students, whom he revered. And he asked him to marry his daughter after she agreed. She had memorised the Qur'an and studied the *tafsir* and learned every word in the Qur'an. And she asked him once. I know the *ayah* of,

$$رَبَّنَآ ءَاتِنَا فِى ٱلدُّنْيَا حَسَنَةً وَفِى ٱلْءَاخِرَةِ حَسَنَةً وَقِنَا عَذَابَ ٱلنَّارِ$$

This is, by the way, the most comprehensive *du'a'*. She said, "I know what is *ḥasanatul akhirah*." The supplication means: Our Lord, grant us a goodly reward in this life and a goodly reward in the hereafter and protect us against the fire of hell. She said, "I know what is a goodly reward of the hereafter. It is none other than *Jannah*. But what is the goodly reward of this life?" He said, "*A good wife.*" If you are blessed with a good wife, that is *ḥasanatud-dunya*. Everything will be set straight. Everything will be upright if you are blessed to have a good wife. In Surah Ali Imran verse 185 Allah (s.w.t.) said:

$$كُلُّ نَفْسٍ ذَآئِقَةُ ٱلْمَوْتِ ۗ وَإِنَّمَا تُوَفَّوْنَ أُجُورَكُمْ يَوْمَ ٱلْقِيَٰمَةِ ۖ فَمَن زُحْزِحَ عَنِ ٱلنَّارِ وَأُدْخِلَ ٱلْجَنَّةَ فَقَدْ فَازَ ۗ وَمَا ٱلْحَيَوٰةُ ٱلدُّنْيَآ إِلَّا مَتَٰعُ ٱلْغُرُورِ ﴿١٨٥﴾$$

Every soul will taste death, and you will only be given your [full] compensation on the Day of Resurrection. So he who is drawn away from the Fire and admitted to Paradise has attained [his desire]. *And what is the life of this world except the enjoyment of delusion.*

Basically, this *dunya* is about a swift and transient enjoyment—*ad-dunya mata'ah*. And the best enjoyment ever in this life is to have a good wife. This is evident in a sound hadith of the Prophet (s.a.w.):

> The world is enjoyment and the best enjoyment in the world is a righteous wife.

Ṣaḥīḥ Muslim 1467

Those of you who are married may know what I am talking about, and those who are not married yet, you keep contemplating thinking about this moment. And *wallāhi*, this is the greatest feeling ever. If I tell you it is even greater than having an intimate relationship, you would have to try it out first in order to judge it yourself. Imagine, when you wake up at night. And you wake up your wife and you both make *wudu'* and you pray *tahajjud* together and you lead her in the prayer. Then you make *qunut* in the *witr*, both of you are flying in heaven. This is something that you got to experience on your own in order to know what I am talking about. In the hadith, the Prophet (s.a.w.) said:

> May Allah have mercy on a man who gets up at night and prays, and awakens his wife; if she refuses, he should sprinkle water on her face. May Allah have mercy on a woman who gets up at night and prays, and awakens her husband; if he refuses, she would sprinkle water on his face.

Sunan Abi Dawud 1308

May Allah have mercy on her husband who would wake up at night to pray, even to pray two *raka'ah* for *tahajjud*. And then he wants his wife also to achieve such goodness, so he says, "Honey. Get up, pray two or four *raka'ah* of *tahajjud*." She is too sleepy. You know, it took her a while to put the kids to sleep in the early morning. She has to prepare them for school, she says, "I'm too tired, Habibi. He says, "*Bismillāh, Bismillāh* only two *raka'ah*."

Whenever she's too sleepy, the Prophet (s.a.w.) says:

نَضَحَ فِي وَجْهِهَا الْمَاءَ

If I may make it with my two fingers and sprinkle them.

This is meaningful. It is not to pour a bucket of water on her and say the Shaykh said so. This is because some people—they will misinterpret what I am saying and they will put me in trouble. There is a hadith where the Prophet (s.a.w.) said, if you see a bad dream, what are you supposed to do? Turn to your left side and blow thrice, not spit. Blow thrice and say *aʿūdhubillāhiminashayṭānirrajīm*. So the sister attended the class and one day when she was asleep next to her husband, who was a butcher. She sees a bad dream. And he wakes up being showered with the spit. "Are you out of your mind?" She said. "No, this is what the Shaykh said." "Shaykh said you spit on your husband, who's a butcher?" Shaykh didn't say that. It is to blow thrice. Not to spit so the Prophet (s.a.w.) said that you may wet your hand and wipe over her face, or splash a little bit of water in order to wake her up so that she will join you for *tahajjud*. And also the other way around, may Allah have mercy on a woman who wakes up at night to pray and then awakens her husband too. And if he is not showing any compliance. She will do the same. Sprinkle some water. Do not shower him while he is asleep. Then said Shaykh said so. If they both wake up and they pray even two *rakaʿah*, they will be recorded before Allah. If you are not married yet, it is not something to be ashamed of, OK. Keep thinking about it and anticipating this moment *wallāhi*, it is the most pleasant thing in life. To get up at night with your spouse. Not just have something in common. Pray *taḥajjud* in *jama'ah*. Even as I said, if it is only two *raka'ah* and you pray the *witr*. If you are married and you have not done it yet, try it. It will transform your marital relationship. And remember, it is all because the Prophet (s.a.w.) said *raḥimah*—may Allah have *mercy* on us so the Prophet (s.a.w.) is praying for the couple who will do as mentioned earlier, and that is the hadith.

Do you know that when I mentioned earlier that marriage is one of the greatest acts of worship, in addition to what is mentioned earlier in the sound hadith, the Prophet (s.a.w.) said that an intimate relationship with your spouse is also an act of worship? And you will be rewarded for that. And it is not any lesser than the rest of the *'ibadat*. The *ṣaḥabah* were introduced to that for the first time, so they were like their eyes were grown wild. "Our Prophet of Allah, how could having sex be considered an act of worship? It's sex." So the Prophet (s.a.w.) said, "What if the person were to commit adultery? Isn't it a sin?" "Yes, it's a major sin." He said similarly for avoiding what is haram and resorting to what is halal. The Almighty Allah will reward him or her for that. *Bud'a* refers to the intimate relationship between a husband and wife. Since we are talking about marriage as an act of worship, not only a means of fulfilling sexual desire and forming a family and having a line of kids to carry your name I am reminded of Sa'ad ibn Abi Waqqas (r.a.). He (r.a.) is one of the 10 heaven-bound companions and he was also Prophet Muhammad's uncle. He was severely ill that he thought he was not going to make it and he was going to die. The Prophet (s.a.w.) paid him a visit. So he said, "O' Rasulullah. You know that I have plenty of money." He was a multimillionaire. "And I only have one single daughter. So all this money, she doesn't need it. Can I give it away?" He (s.a.w.) said "No." Then he asked, "Can I give away two-thirds of it?" He (s.a.w.) said "No." "Half of it?" "No." "One-third of it?" He (s.a.w.) said, "One-third and it's still too much." Then he (s.a.w.) remarked saying, "You will be rewarded for whatever you spend for Allah's sake even if it were a morsel which you put in your wife's mouth." (From Ṣaḥiḥ al-Bukhari 56) Including even what you put in the mouth of your wife when you feed her and say, "Honey taste this. Take this from me." This is an act of worship and you only be rewarded for it. Not only when you take her for *ʿumrah* or for *ḥajj*. When you go out for dinner, when you go vacationing, as long as it is a halal vacation *Mashā'Allāh* —your wife is wearing her hijab, you both are praying on time and eating halal food and you are earning from halal. The spending that you spend on her and on your children is an act of charity. And it is rewarded more than given to people with whom you have no relationship. School tuitions—*ṣadaqah*. Medication—*ṣadaqah*. Clothes, coats, jewellery, ornaments—all of these are ṣadaqah. The sisters reading might say, "Shaykh, put emphasis on this, please!" Remember that you will be rewarded for all of that. Only in Islam, do you find that because it values the relationship between the husband and wife. So the relationship between them is based on compassion, respect, and love, not on competition because nowadays some people perceive their life-long partner as a rival. *Subḥānallāh.*

Legal Status of Marriage in Islam

Before getting into the serious business, such as the marriage, the marriage contract and the requirements, the pillars, the conditions, and the engagement, we want to know whether marriage is *wajib* or merely recommended. There is a general consensus among all the scholars that marriage is *mandub* meaning recommended. *Mustahab* on the other hand means it is highly recommended and rewarded. Some of the earlier men perceived it, even as compulsory, whenever they can afford the means. Recapping what the Prophet (s.a.w.) has encouraged young people—men and women, whoever can afford to get married because it is better with regards to lowering your gaze guarding your chastity and so on. And because Allah (s.w.t.) stated in Surah an-Nur verse 32:

وَأَنكِحُوا۟ ٱلْأَيَـٰمَىٰ مِنكُمْ وَٱلصَّـٰلِحِينَ مِنْ عِبَادِكُمْ وَإِمَآئِكُمْ ۚ إِن يَكُونُوا۟ فُقَرَآءَ يُغْنِهِمُ ٱللَّهُ مِن فَضْلِهِۦ ۗ وَٱللَّهُ وَٰسِعٌ عَلِيمٌ ﴿٣٢﴾

And marry the unmarried among you and the righteous among your male slaves and female slaves. If they should be poor, Allāh will enrich them from His bounty, and Allāh is all-Encompassing and Knowing.

Here Allah (s.w.t.) commanded us to financially assist those who cannot afford to get married. He (s.w.t.) promised that even if they are poor, Allah will enrichen them out of His bounty. Look at the meaning of this verse, because we are going back to the area shortly after I compare this verse and another verse in Surah at-Tawbah. Pay close attention to it. And here is *ayah*:

يَـٰٓأَيُّهَا ٱلَّذِينَ ءَامَنُوٓا۟ إِنَّمَا ٱلْمُشْرِكُونَ نَجَسٌ فَلَا يَقْرَبُوا۟ ٱلْمَسْجِدَ ٱلْحَرَامَ بَعْدَ عَامِهِمْ هَـٰذَا ۚ وَإِنْ خِفْتُمْ عَيْلَةً فَسَوْفَ يُغْنِيكُمُ ٱللَّهُ مِن فَضْلِهِۦٓ إِن شَآءَ ۚ إِنَّ ٱللَّهَ عَلِيمٌ حَكِيمٌ ﴿٢٨﴾

O' you who have believed, indeed the polytheists are unclean, so let them not approach al-Masjid al-Haram after this, their [final] year. And if you fear privation, Allah will enrich you from His bounty if He wills. Indeed, Allah is Knowing and Wise.

When we travel through the Qur'an and go to chapter 9 verse 28, there is an *ayah* which is irrelevant to our topic. It has nothing to do with marriage. Allah (s.w.t.) in the 9th year after the migration revealed Surah at-Tawbah. The Prophet (s.a.w.) sent 'Ali ibn Abi Talib and Abu Bakr as-Siddiq to perform *hajj* for the first time. And he (s.a.w.) performed *hajj* the next year. He said Makkah is only for Muslims. Upon hearing that, the people of Makkah were really worried. Because Makkah as a town does not produce anything, does not have oil, and does not manufacture anything, it earns its income through selling idols and tourism. So now it is only for Muslims, what should they depend on for their economic growth? So Allah (s.w.t.) said:

So He assures them, and if you're afraid of poverty, don't worry. Allah will enrichen them out of His bounty **if He wills**.

Insha' means He may or He may not will. But in verse 32 Surah an-Nur, when Allah (s.w.t.) says you guys help the youth who want to get married. The singles, who are not married, even if they are poor, have been to get married, He (s.w.t.) said:

> If they should be poor, Allah will enrich them from His bounty, and Allah is all-Encompassing and Knowing.

He (s.w.t.) promised again—Allah will enrichen them out of His bounty. But he did not say *insha'*. What difference does it make here? It is guaranteed. Every time somebody wants to get married in halal, even if they are poor. Allah promises 100% that He will support them, you might wonder how with your limited income? The 'how' is none of your business. It is up to Allah (s.w.t.), who says:

$$وَمَن يَتَّقِ اللَّـهَ يَجْعَل لَّهُ مَخْرَجًا ۝ وَيَرْزُقْهُ مِنْ حَيْثُ لَا يَحْتَسِبُ ۚ وَمَن يَتَوَكَّلْ عَلَى اللَّـهِ فَهُوَ حَسْبُهُ ۚ إِنَّ اللَّـهَ بَالِغُ أَمْرِهِ ۚ قَدْ جَعَلَ اللَّـهُ لِكُلِّ شَيْءٍ قَدْرًا ۝$$

"And whoever fears Allah - He will make for him a way out. And will provide for him from where he does not expect. And whoever relies upon Allah - then He is sufficient for him. Indeed, Allah will accomplish His purpose. Allah has already set for everything a [decreed] extent."

Surah at-Ṭalaq:2-3

Whosoever fears Allah and keeps his duty to him, Allah (s.w.t.) will deliver him out of every hardship and will provide for him from means which he could never anticipate.

Diving into the main point on *hukm* of marriage in Islam, in reality, it undergoes the five legal decrees in Islam. Everything with regards to the dos and don'ts could be *wajib* (obligatory), *mustahab* or *sunnah* (recommended), then halal (permissible), *makruh* (disliked) or haram (forbidden). Can we give examples of those five legal *ahkam*? What is *wajib*? *Salah*. Eating from halal. Recommended? To drink with the right hand. Sit down whenever you want to drink. To give *salam* to Muslims whenever you meet them. To give *salam* is recommended, but when somebody says a *salam* to you responding to that salam is *wajib*. Halal is everything in life other than what is forbidden. Drinking water, drinking juice, lying down, and wearing clothes—these are halal. Give me an example of *makruh*. Divorce? Not necessarily because sometimes divorce may be prescribed. You know, it is not always *makruh*. To drink or to eat while he is standing is *makruh*. An example of haram—drinking wine, eating pork, and wearing silk for men. So these are the five *aḥkam* in Islam.

1.   W*ajib* or *fard* (obligatory)

2.   *Mustahab* (recommended)

3.   Halal (permissible)

4.   *Makruh* (disliked)

5.   *Haram* (forbidden)

Marriage could be one of the five. Let me draw you a situation:

"I'm a young man. *Alḥamdulillāh* graduated. I have a decent job. I'm making a very good income. *Mashā'Allāh* , I have a house. However, I fear for myself. I have the desire."

So then marriage in this case is obligatory or *wajib*. *Alḥamdulillāh*, you don't have any hindrances and you have all the means. Go ahead and get married. It is *wajib*. It may be *mustahab* in the case of a person who is pursuing further education and does not have any interest whatsoever and life is not tempting him. He is also not afraid of falling in the haram and he is busy day and night, so it remains the original condition which is *mustahab* or halal. But do you know when marriage can become *haram*? It is when somebody knows that he cannot take care of his wife but he proceeds towards marriage. Or somebody has a disease which is like for instance, STD—sexually transmitted disease. It is haram for him or her to marry because he or she will infect the other. So we cannot just stay with one *ḥukm* in every case. It is either halal or haram or *wajib* depending on what fits your personal condition. But generally speaking, the *ṣaḥabah*, *at-tabiʿin* and the *ʿulamaʾ* perceived marriage as highly recommended.

Waliyy

The Prophet (s.a.w.) said in one hadith:

> "When someone with whose religion and character you are satisfied asks your daughter in marriage, accede to his request. If you do not do so there will be temptation in the earth and extensive corruption." Tirmidhi transmitted it.

Mishkat al-Maṣabiḥ 3090

Now this hadith is addressing the guardians. For example, me as a father or as a *waliyy* or as a guardian. I happen to be a guardian not only for my girls but for many Muslim revert girls from the States, from Canada, and from all over Europe. Whenever a girl, one of my students says, "Shaykh, I want you to be my guardian." I would say yes on one condition—I exercise all my rights as a guardian. This means I would consider you my daughter. Then I will love for you how I love for my daughter. And I would not approve anything to you that I would not approve for my daughter. It is one of the girls who found a guy whom she wanted to marry and she explained that this person studies Arabic and Qur'an. So I asked her where is this brother located at? She said he is in the UK. So I met him in the UK. I gave him my phone number for us to meet. I was giving some talks there. And when we met, I investigated because, you know, whatever you read online and on the matrimonial websites, it is 99% fake. They think somebody would say, you know, "I'm a short guy and I'm fat and I have a big belly and I don't have a degree and I'm broke." Of course everybody will perceive themselves like Amitabh Bachchan. And likewise with the girls. There is nothing similar to a meeting in person, gathering information from people who know the person first-hand, and so on. So when I met him, I said, "*Mashā'Allāh* , what do you do for a living?" He said, "I'm not working, Shaykh." "Why not?" He said because I'm studying. "I thought you were 31? Why are you studying? So what is your major?" He said, "I didn't go to college." *Mashā'Allāh* , 31 and you barely have a high school degree. He did not even finish it by. Furthering the conversation, I asked, "So what are you studying?" He said, "I study in Arabic and Qur'an. I want to become *dai'e*." So I said, "*Mashā'Allāh*! So you speak Arabic now?" He said no. "So what are you studying? Have you memorised the Qur'an? How much Qur'an you have memorised?" Nothing of what he has written to her is true. He does not know Arabic, he is not working, and he does not have a degree. Then I asked so how do you live? He said my parents support me. I said, you know, the girl whom I happened to be her guardian is a revert. She is studying with me and she is working to support herself. She is paying for her own rent, accommodation, lodging, food and everything. *Inshā'Allāh*, when you both get married, whom do you expect will support the family? So he said, *Allah will support*. When he said that, I said, "*Habibi*, take a hike. Right away." This is a very irresponsible person. He does not even show any interest to be a man. And I have many cases where the man from the beginning enjoyed the free ride. The wife is working, the wife is earning and he is staying at home. "Yeah, I help. I'm doing the dishes." *Mashā'Allāh*, not good enough. The wife after thirty years of working and providing for the family, said, "I want a divorce." She said, "Shaykh. I needed to be with a man. I feel like I am the man of the house." And she is right. Allah (s.w.t.) created everyone for certain tasks, OK? So when I see somebody who is serious, *Mashā'Allāh*, he is working two jobs, two shifts, working hard and attending classes. He has a degree and he is still broke or he cannot afford to live in a decent place. But I have the means and she is my daughter. I will help you out. Why? Because you deserve the help. But when a loser proposes to my daughter? Of course not. No way. I am not going to bring another person to the house who would enjoy the free ride, eat and drink like a pet. So the Prophet (s.a.w.) says to the guardians—the father, uncle, the man who was in charge. If somebody proposes to your girl, your daughter, the girl under your guardianship, whom you trust, INVESTIGATE. The Prophet (s.a.w.) is addressing the guardians because only the guardians can find out. People fall in love. Even in fake or pseudo love situations online without meeting in person. I was invited to counsel a case where the wife is insisting on divorce. She said when he proposed to me in front of my parents, he said that he is working at this particular place. His earning is this amount and he has a house and he speaks seven languages. *Mashā'Allāh* . Then after we got married, none of that was true. He barely speaks Arabic and that is his mother tongue. And he admitted all of that. He admitted that he lied to her in the beginning. Allah (s.w.t.) ordered that there should be a guardian to do the investigation. Not to say, "I give you my girl or my daughter in marriage?" But to investigate and find out whether this person is fulfilling these qualities. Look at this with regards to *deen* and *amanah.* If you think because you see this guy *Mashā'Allāh* wearing a beard and a turban and memorising Qur'an and attending classes, it is sufficient, no! Not on my watch. So what is good for your daughter is to see how the person deals with people beginning with his parents, siblings, and neighbours at work, and at school.

When I gather this information and they say he is super nice, then *alhamdulillāh*. Is it possible to see a person who is going to the masjid on a regular basis and attending classes but is violent, abusive, and rude to his parents? It happens a lot. There are two things that the Prophet (s.a.w.) did not neglect which are *dinahu wa khuluqahu* (religion and character) as mentioned in the hadith (Mishkat al-Maṣabiḥ 3090). When I was young, across from my house, there was a guy who would not miss a prayer and wear a beard. But *Subḥānallāh* every day I hear him and I see him beating his wife. She cries and she screams. Then when they see him in the masjid, *Mashā'Allāh* he was like an angel; as if he has not done a crime right now before coming to the masjid. Some people have the ability to wear a mask. A girl will not find out on her own whether this guy is a monster or an angel. It is the guardian who would have to investigate. And if you find out that the guy fulfils these conditions—can support a family, is religiously committed so he prays on time but only one thing lacks—he smokes. When I am asked live on air that the guy is proposing to my daughter smokes—no means no. He promises that he will quit. Whenever he quits and whenever it is confirmed he does not smoke at all, then we may consider him. When you compromise on this matter then after marriage, you might find yourself saying, "I cannot live with him because he promised he will quit but he did not." This is because he was not even planning to do so. If he was serious, he would have done it before getting married. Al-Ḥasan al-Basri (r.a.h.), when a man asked him and consulted him: There are a lot of people proposing to my daughter, to whom shall I give her in marriage? He (r.a.h.) said, "Give her in marriage to the man whom, if he loves her, he would honour her and in case that there is no love no more, he would still treat her well and not wrong her because he is a man of manners." 'Umar ibn al-Khaṭṭab (r.a.) heard two people talking to each other. One of them was making a recommendation saying, "Muhammad— Yeah, I know him very well. He's a very good man, *Mashā'Allāh* . He's a man of his word. Very honest. And you know, he will be the best to your daughter, so he said, "*Mashā'Allāh* , you know him?" He said, "I know very well." He asked, "Is he your neighbour? Does he live next to you?" He said no. "Oh, maybe you travel together?" "Oh, no, no, no. We never travelled together." "Did you deal with him in business?" He said no. So the other person said, "So how do you know that he's a good man? Perhaps you see him going to the masjid?" He said. "Yes." He said. "That is not sufficient." In order to judge whether a person is a truly good person or not, check him out in dealing with money— business and trade, taking loans and payments. And ask his neighbours. Because a person cannot conceal his reality all the time, his neighbours would know better. His co-workers, classmates and teachers. And also in travelling a long journey, because the person cannot conceal his reality for so long, he will be exposed. A genuine person on the other hand, in every condition—everyone would say, "*Mashā'Allāh,* he's a nice guy." So, recite *basmalah* and accept such a proposal. So look at the character. Whether he is loving, patient, or modest. Chemistry is very important and that is why to begin with if the girl is not happy with her suitor, I did not say just OK and that is it. If she is not truly happy, do not proceed towards this marriage. This is a true chemistry and it is not permissible for a guardian to give a girl who is under his guardianship in marriage to anyone against her will, even if he is super nice. There must be *ijab* and *qabul.* Look for one whose hardworking, dedicated and ambitious. Imam Abu Hanifah is the most strict in this regard. He considers something called *kafa'ah.* So he does not approve that a girl who is hardworking and has a degree marrying somebody who is a loser, just because he is religious. No, there must be some sort of compatibility between them with their families or individuals. And this is a piece of general advice for you sisters and for us, the brothers. If you keep waiting for Mr. Right—there will be no Mr. Right. In order to have Mr Right, you have to be Mrs. Right. And the same goes for the brothers. So we have to compromise. You will not find a person who is 100% fulfilling all the requirements, right? In the States, there is a magazine, if you happen to visit or live there, *School Horizon* which is issued by a big organisation. So every week, there will be the typical matrimonial ad. You know, such and such family, looking for a suitor for their fair, slim and tall daughter. The suitor must be a medical doctor, an American citizen, tall, and have a house and a car. Have this and that, and by the end, *religious*. So in reality you can dream of whatever you want. But what would really last a man of his word, a man of honour, a man who would respect her—not because of her father, not because of her family? Because of her, because of who she is. Look for the one who has good relations with his family members. Particularly the parents and the rest of the community. Whose duty it is to gather the information? The girl's guardian. This is his duty before Allah (s.w.t.).

Choosing the Right Spouse

It has been mentioned before regarding what type of person you may consider their proposals, in terms of on what basis, and what you should look for in a man. Now, it is time for the brothers to consider what the Prophet (s.a.w.) has said in respect of seeking a wife and a life mate.

I am sure everyone must have heard about this hadith: The four qualities you should consider when you want to marry a woman. What if I say this hadith is one of the most misunderstood ahadith? What does the hadith say? The hadith is a sound hadith and it is collected by Imam Bukhari and Muslim and others. It is a highly profound hadith.

Narrated Abu Hurayrah:

The Prophet (s.a.w.) said, "A woman is married for four things, i.e., her wealth, her family status, her beauty and her religion. So you should marry the religious woman (otherwise) you will be a losers."

Ṣaḥiḥ al-Bukhari 5090

Another hadith is narrated as such:

It was narrated from 'Abdullah bin Amr that:

The Prophet (s.a.w.) said: "Do not marry women for their beauty for it may lead to their doom. Do not marry them for their wealth, for it may lead them to fall into sin. Rather, marry them for their religion. A black slave woman with piercings who is religious is better."

Sunan Ibn Majah 1859

Criteria one to three are easy to understand. Then when it comes to the final segment where the Prophet says, "So you should marry the religious woman (otherwise) you will be losers."

This is where most of the brothers misunderstand. When they read the hadith, they would understand that they have to only focus on one thing which is being religious and disregard the other three qualities." This is not the correct understanding. Rather, it means these are the very prominent qualities which every man or every Muslim would like to have. A Muslim man should like to marry a woman who is pretty and belonging to a good family. What if she is wealthy and her family are wealthy? This is also a plus. The Prophet (s.a.w.) did not say to disregard all of that and only look for a woman who is religious. Rather, the Prophet (s.a.w.) means the following: The four qualities are beauty, wealth, family and lineage, and religious commitment. If you find a girl who has these four qualities, give me her phone number. She is the one. Right away do not waste the chance. Seize the opportunity. But for example, after looking for years, you could only find a woman who has three qualities, not all of four. Then one of the three qualities must be the *deen*. "I found one with only two qualities. She's beautiful." Then she must be also religiously committed. This means that the *deen* should be an essential ingredient and component in decision making. "I chose this woman because she is *Mashā'Allāh* , she is a professional and she is religious. She belongs to a very righteous family or the family, who consider themselves *Sayyid* or *Sharif*." "What about her?" "She is *Mashā'Allāh* religious." There must be an essential component whenever you make the decision. But if you find a girl who is *Alḥamdulillāh* besides being pretty and belonging to a good family and driving a Lamborghini, she is also religious, then you are a winner. Why waste your time? Propose right away and follow the procedures. That is the meaning behind فَاظْفَـرْ بِـذَاتِ الدَّيـنِ تَرِبَـتْ يَـدَاَ

If so it happens that you have the three qualities without the *deen*, in most cases such marriage does not last unless you yourself are willing to compromise on account of your religious commitment. She is a liberal. She is outgoing and she used to have friends who are boys from here and there and from college time. They go out together. Are you willing to permit that? Are you willing to see your wife very liberal going out with men and not wearing hijab, not worrying about offering her *ṣalah*? What about later on when you have children? How are you going to raise them? How are you going to decide with regard to every matter pertaining to their future if you are not on the same page? So the *deen* should be an essential component in the decision making. This is what is meant by the Prophet (s.a.w.) in the end of the hadith.

The following hadith emphasises what I mentioned earlier. It is very important that whenever a girl accepts the proposal of a man or whenever a man is looking for a girl to marry, the look is very important. You do not have to accept any person with whom you are not convinced. Who does not please you whenever you look at him, do not marry him. Do not say you know, "But he prays." "But *Mashā'Allāh* he is active in *da'wah*." He has to look nice and smell nice to you. He has to impress you. If not, please back off. Maybe he will find somebody else who would perceive him as smart and nice. This applies the same to the girl.

In the past, in a marriage, a man would not even get to see the woman until the time of consummating their marriage. And the woman would not even know anything about this man other than maybe his name in the past and until today, in some areas, but this is not permissible. The Prophet (s.a.w.) said to his companions:

$$انْظُرْ إِلَيْهَا فَإِنَّهُ أَحْرَى أَنْ يُؤْدَمَ بَيْنَكُمَا$$

Bakr bin Abdullah Al-Muzani narrated that :

Al-Mughirah bin Shuʻbah proposed to a woman, so the Prophet said: "Look at her, for indeed that is more likely to make things better between the two of you."

Jamiʻ at-Tirmidhi 1087

When one of the companions got engaged, the Prophet (s.a.w.) would ask, "Did you see her?" He said no. This is because it was the norm at that time. He (s.a.w.) then said, "No. You need to go and look at her. This is more worthy for a better relationship between you and her." And it goes both ways. So she has to see him and he has to see her, please, without makeup. Recently, there are so many divorce cases, and also *wallāhi* lawsuits. Why? Because the guy was so impressed with the beauty of the girl. And then the next morning, after consummating their marriage, he was shocked to see his brother next to him. A completely different person. Their marriage did not even last for one day. It is OK to wear light makeup, but the first meeting should be your original self. This is so that he would know who you are and you would know who he is without modification, without changing your original look. So the Prophet (s.a.w.) said to look at her for indeed, that is more likely to make things better between both of you.

The Pursuit

As far as the pursuit, where to look for a spouse? This is for a man who is looking for a wife or a girl who is looking for a husband. Obviously, masjid is the number one place to spread the word in. *Halaqah*, the shaykh, the teachers, conventions, and gatherings like that because you will need people who have something in common with you who share the same interest. Or maybe family friends. Is the online matrimonial service and the Internet a safe place or a reliable place to find a suitor? The answer is absolutely not. Give me a single guarantee that what you read is authentic. You have no idea whether what he or she has introduced themselves within their bio is true. There is no guarantee whatsoever, especially when you guys live far away from each other. You might live in different countries and you only meet on the day of the *nikah*. The man is in France and the woman is in the UK. Just like that marriages take place. Personally, I have attended many of these events where the bride and groom have never met before. This is not sufficient. It is very deceiving and it is very hurtful. Many youths including us when we were young, we are opposing the idea of arranged marriage. What is an arranged marriage? It is when the family or family friends propose somebody who is within our circle. So that person would say, "No I will make my own decision. I will make my own choice when I meet Mr. Right or miss right. The person who impresses me." Consider the family arrangement or the arranged marriage. This is an opportunity for you. Maybe you will like her or him. Maybe you will find them the best suitor. You would never know. But in either case, you have to know the boundaries in recommending. You do not force or put pressure on the person to marry the candidate. Your job is just to recommend as a parent, as a guardian, as a senior person, and so on. Then if you find something in common or chemistry between them—*love at first sight*. The first meeting and that happens, and this is acknowledged and we say Islam actually recognises that. But how should you go about it? Through the girl's *waliyy*. The girl belongs to a family. Allah (s.a.w.) says in the Qur'an,

$$ وَلَيْسَ ٱلْبِرُّ بِأَن تَأْتُوا۟ ٱلْبُيُوتَ مِن ظُهُورِهَا وَلَـٰكِنَّ $$

$$ ٱلْبِرَّ مَنِ ٱتَّقَىٰ ۗ وَأْتُوا۟ ٱلْبُيُوتَ مِنْ أَبْوَٰبِهَا ۚ وَٱتَّقُوا۟ ٱللَّهَ $$

$$ لَعَلَّكُمْ تُفْلِحُونَ ۝١٨٩ ... $$

...And it is not righteousness to enter houses from the back, but righteousness is [in] one who fears Allah. And enter houses from their doors. And fear Allah that you may succeed.

(al-Baqarah 2:189)

Houses have doors—front and back as well as windows. Only thieves break into the house from the windows, but honourable guests would ring the bell and ask for the man of the house. Introduce yourself and state your intention of making the *waliyy* and your parents meet. "I heard that you have a daughter and I'm interested in getting to know her." Tell the *waliyy* your name, from which family you belong, what occupation you have and what level of education you are at. Another option might be, if we live in a community where there is an imam and a masjid who can actually manage to introduce you to the family or family friends, *Alhamdulillāh*, that would be a lot easier. But to date without the knowledge of their family, and to go out together without establishing a legal relationship is the wrong beginning and it is haram. Some religiously committed girls would say, "I would rather meet him outside in order to get to know him before he would visit my parents' house, and proposes to me. This is the wrong beginning. Is dating permissible even with the intention of getting married? No, it is not permissible.

What is halal is halal and it is obvious and clear. The same goes for what is haram. It is haram and obvious and clear.

$$\text{إِنَّ الْحَلَالَ بَيِّنٌ، وَإِنَّ الْحَرَامَ بَيِّنٌ}$$

"That which is lawful is clear and that which is unlawful is clear,...

Hadith 6, 40 Hadith an-Nawawi

Come to the houses from the front doors. Reflect on at what Allah (s.w.t.) says in Surah al-Baqarah verse 189. Success comes to those who acknowledge their emotions, fulfill their obligations towards Allah, and maintain a strong adherence to what is permissible and forbidden in accordance with His teachings. So when a man visits your house and proposes to you and it seems that you are interested to find out more about this person, it is your guardian's responsibility to find out about his manners, his attitude, and his seriousness from outside through investigation. Then you may wonder, what about me? What are the questions I should concern myself with? What should I ask my suitor?

First and foremost, your concern is *deen*. If the suitor treats his *deen* in an insignificant manner even though he is nice, you should say no, thank you from the beginning. If someone lacks fear of Allah (s.w.t.) and fails to maintain a strong relationship with Him, it is unlikely that they will exhibit God-fearing behaviour towards their spouse or children.

This is lacking honesty. This type of person, when makes promises that they would start practising the *deen,* would never fulfil it. This is because if it is not coming from within, it cannot be sustained. This is because we are a servant of Allah (s.w.t.) and our *ṣalah* is the most important pillar of the *deen.* If he does not understand this, then he might not change for you. It is important to figure out whether his family, parents and siblings are also practising or not. I have a story about this. When I wanted to get married, I phoned my Shaykh. At that time, I wanted to marry an American girl. I was so close to marrying her. But I consulted my Shaykh first and he said before you make the decision, look who is going to be the maternal uncles of your children. Once I looked into who was going to be my in-laws, I changed my mind, right away. They do have an influence and effect on your children because you cannot avoid meeting them. You are not going to boycott their family and isolate her from her family. Of course, we are talking about the best scenario and the most ideal situation, if you really want to enjoy a happy Islamic marital relationship.

Other than that, do not hesitate to discuss issues with regard to children. Some brothers only talked to their wives about this after they get married. The wife would express her intention to delay having children for a period of three to four years. Consequently, the husband raises a question, wondering why she did not disclose this information earlier. He emphasises that if he had known about her plans beforehand, he would not have shown interest. He clarifies that he desires to have children as soon as possible, once they are blessed with marriage. So things like that must be very clear.

To inquire about finance is also important. Ask questions such questions: What do you do for a living? Do you have a place to live in? Rental or do you own it? Who else are you supporting? This is to set things clear of your financial expectations.

There is another thing that is really important. It is very common in some cultures that a person marries so that his wife will serve his family. From the Islamic perspective, it is really problematic because most of the time, the woman ends up feeling that she has been hired as a maid but without monetary payment, only compensated with food and drink. This is not permissible. Every woman, every wife is entitled to her own house and she is the queen of the house. So it is OK to be open from the beginning and ask if you are going to live with the parents, or with the family at the family house or you are going to live separately. You have to be very clear in this regard.

In some cases, your suitor's job requires him to travel a lot. Ask him how often he travels. Maybe he has to pursue his higher education for four or five years so you both will be apart for a while. That might not suit you. Others do not mind and do not have a problem with that due to their financial situation. It really depends on the individual. But you must be crystal clear with your future spouse regarding all these aspects we discussed. Maybe the woman has not finished studying just yet. But since the man does not mind, so it would not be a problem. That must be concluded in writing. Another scenario is a woman who is interested in pursuing postgraduate education, and she says, "I don't mind getting married right now, but I would be interested in doing my Masters and PhD." If he does not find this a problem, he must remember that that is a condition he stipulated on himself. He has agreed to such a term. The Prophet (s.a.w.) said in a hadith:

إِنَّ أَحَقَّ الشَّرْطِ أَنْ يُوفَى بِهِ مَا اسْتَحْلَلْتُمْ بِهِ الْفُرُوجَ

The most worthy condition which must be fulfilled is that which makes sexual intercourse lawful. In the narration transmitted by Ibn Muthanna (instead of the word" condition") it is" conditions".

Ṣaḥiḥ Muslim 1418

This means that if you did not agree to this condition from the beginning, she would have turned down your proposal. You fully understand that therefore you agree to the condition. It is pertinent that agreeing means you would commit to the condition wholeheartedly. For example, there is a situation where the condition is set by the parents. So the father says, "Son, as long as you are living in KL, we don't mind. But if you're migrating elsewhere—France, Germany—anywhere, my daughter is not going." You agreed to that stipulated condition therefore you must fulfil whatever requirements are needed.

Next is health-related questions. Health is a very important aspect that should be discussed with full honesty by both parties. Firstly, we have established that a person with STDs should not get married in the first place. Secondly, discuss possible or existing chronic illnesses that the suitor might have which may affect the livelihood of the couple in the future. This includes when somebody is diabetic, hyper or hypotensive. Or when somebody has some liver issues or renal failure This is because the person from the beginning may decline the proposal and say, "*Wallāhi*, I'm not interested, may Allah (s.w.t.) give you *shifa'*." Fertility is also an important issue to be talked about especially when you are planning to have a family. This can be investigated based on the family's medical history. So all of that should be taken into consideration and discussed with full honesty.

Istikharah

Now that everything is transparent—you have inquired the important questions, there comes the role of *istikharah*.

The right order as we discussed is firstly *istisharah* (consultation and investigation). Then *istikharah*. This is because *istikharah*, which is done through the prayer of *istikharah*, should be based on information that you collected, not on vague situations. For example, as a man, you are interested in marrying a woman after knowing the important things about her. You feel she is going to be the love of your life and the best suitor for you. Would this be the same with the woman? Not necessarily. Allah (s.w.t.) knows best. This means that you have to consult Allah (s.w.t.) regarding this marriage, by offering two *raka'at* with the intention of praying *istikharah*. You can even pray the supplementary of any prayer: *Zuhr*, *Maghrib*, *'Isha'* and you combine two intentions. Then, after you conclude, raise your hand and recite this supplication. Maybe you do not memorise it by heart. It does not matter, read it from your phone, or your notepad. The *du'a'* goes:

اللَّهُمَّ إِنِّي أَسْتَخِيرُكَ بِعِلْمِكَ وَأَسْتَقْدِرُكَ بِقُدْرَتِكَ، وَأَسْأَلُكَ مِنْ فَضْلِكَ الْعَظِيمِ، فَإِنَّكَ تَقْدِرُ وَلاَ أَقْدِرُ وَتَعْلَمُ وَلاَ أَعْلَمُ وَأَنْتَ عَلاَّمُ الْغُيُوبِ، اللَّهُمَّ إِنْ كُنْتَ تَعْلَمُ أَنَّ هَذَا الأَمْرَ خَيْرٌ لِي فِي دِينِي وَمَعَاشِي وَعَاقِبَةِ أَمْرِي ـ أَوْ قَالَ عَاجِلِ أَمْرِي وَآجِلِهِ ـ فَاقْدُرْهُ لِي وَيَسِّرْهُ لِي ثُمَّ بَارِكْ لِي فِيهِ، وَإِنْ كُنْتَ تَعْلَمُ أَنَّ هَذَا الأَمْرَ شَرٌّ لِي فِي دِينِي وَمَعَاشِي وَعَاقِبَةِ أَمْرِي ـ أَوْ قَالَ فِي عَاجِلِ أَمْرِي وَآجِلِهِ ـ فَاصْرِفْهُ عَنِّي وَاصْرِفْنِي عَنْهُ، وَاقْدُرْ لِي الْخَيْرَ حَيْثُ كَانَ ثُمَّ أَرْضِنِي بِهِ

O' Allah! I ask guidance from Your knowledge, And Power from Your Might and I ask for Your great blessings. You are capable and I am not. You know and I do not and You know the unseen. O' Allah! If You know that this job is good for my religion and my subsistence and in my Hereafter--(or said: If it is better for my present and later needs)--Then You ordain it for me and make it easy for me to get, And then bless me in it, and if You know that this job is harmful to me In my religion and subsistence and in the Hereafter--(or said: If it is worse for my present and later needs)--Then keep it away from me and let me be away from it. And ordain for me whatever is good for me, And make me satisfied with it.

Ṣaḥiḥ al-Bukhari 1166

O' Allah, if You knew in Your infinite knowledge that this woman is going to be good for me as a wife with regards to my worldly life and hereafter, then make this marriage easy for me and facilitate it for me. But if you know otherwise, then look at the beautiful phrase:

... ،فَاصْرِفْهُ عَنِّي وَاصْرِفْنِي عَنْهُ ...

Then keep it away from me and let me be away from it.

Then take her and her family away from me and take me away from her. Divert us both from each other because sometimes you have established that you are not interested. But the other party is still interested so they put pressure on you so you may yield. Ask Allah (s.w.t.) to give you away from each other. This does not mean that she is inherently bad or you are inherently bad, but it only means that you are not good for each other. Maybe you are good for other couples, for other suitors. Sometimes you may be the best person in the world, and maybe she is the best person in the world as far as religious, status as far as wealth as far as everything, but there is no chemistry or attraction between the two of you. You feel like she is your sister. No, we want you to feel like she is the love of your life, romantically. *Not your sister.* Look at what Allah (s.w.t.) says in this regard in Surah al-Baqarah verse 216:

$$\ldots \text{وَعَسَىٰٓ أَن تَكْرَهُواْ شَيْـًٔا وَهُوَ خَيْرٌ لَّكُمْ وَعَسَىٰٓ أَن تُحِبُّواْ شَيْـًٔا وَهُوَ شَرٌّ لَّكُمْ وَٱللَّهُ يَعْلَمُ وَأَنتُمْ لَا تَعْلَمُونَ ٢١٦}$$

...But perhaps you hate a thing and it is good for you, and perhaps you love a thing and it is bad for you. And Allah knows, while you know not.

It is common that something we dislike may actually be the best for us, but we are unaware of it at the time. Sometimes, this realisation comes later, and unfortunately, there are instances when it dawns upon us when it is too late. Similarly, there are situations where we may have a liking for something that is actually harmful to us. Instead of risking harm to ourselves and others by experimenting, what should we do? We should seek counsel from Allah (s.w.t.), who possesses knowledge of the unseen, the past, the present, and the future. By consulting Him, we can be assured that He will guide us towards what is truly beneficial.

Many people come to me saying, "Shaykh, I want you to pray *istikharah* for me." Well, I'm not the one who is getting married. I'm not the one who would develop the feeling. One of the common misconceptions about *istikharah* in the mind of many Muslims is that you have to pray *istikharah* before you go to sleep. This is because right after you fall asleep, you will see in your dream, the solution to your problem. Allah (s.w.t.) will tell you what to do. This is not necessarily true. You *may* see a dream or you may not. But whatever happens as a result of *istikharah*, this is the consultation and the decision of Allah (s.w.t.). This means that when everything seems to be OK and we are getting along. But when I prayed *istikharah* and she prayed *istikharah*, *Subḥānallāh* Allah (s.w.t.) distanced us. When that happens, it is for the best of both of us. So make sure you pray *istikharah*. If you have performed your *istikharah* prayer once and you are not sure, repeat it several more times until you are convinced. Remember that no one can pray *istikharah* on behalf of another. Sometimes you heard people pay some shaykh to pray *istikharah* for them. This is all fake. It is your feeling that is involved in this situation, not some shaykh's. When you pray *istikharah*, it is to simply go with the flow that Allah (s.w.t.) will guide you. Sometimes everything may seem to be going perfectly, but suddenly things take a turn for the worse. This outcome can be a result of *istikharah*. Alternatively, certain things may be revealed or realised at the last minute, for which we should express gratitude to Allah (s.w.t.). Regardless of what happens, there should be no regrets, as long as *istikharah* has been performed. Additionally, in Surah an-Nisa', verse 19, Allah emphasises that when making decisions, what may appear perfect or wise can actually be either the most correct or the most foolish. He (s.w.t.) says:

...مُّبَيِّنَةٍ ۚ وَعَاشِرُوهُنَّ بِٱلْمَعْرُوفِ ۚ فَإِن كَرِهْتُمُوهُنَّ فَعَسَىٰٓ أَن تَكْرَهُواْ شَيْئًا وَيَجْعَلَ ٱللَّهُ فِيهِ خَيْرًا كَثِيرًا

﴿١٩﴾

...And live with them in kindness. For if you dislike them - perhaps you dislike a thing and Allah makes therein much good.

(an-Nisa' 4:19)

It is entirely possible for us to dislike something that Allah has placed a significant amount of goodness in. Only

Allah truly knows the extent of its goodness. This is precisely why we pray *istikharah*. However, there are instances when *istikharah* becomes invalid or loses its effectiveness. For example, if we have already agreed upon all the aspects of a marriage, such as the dowry, wedding gifts, venue, catering, and *walimah*, and then suddenly you decide to pray *istikharah*, it raises the question of certainty. Why not wait until after consummating the marriage and then perform *istikharah*? It is already too late.

Pray *istikharah* after you have gathered enough information about your suitor. The guardian is doing his homework investigating you so you as a man, should be doing your homework as well to find out the necessary information. Maybe you have met her a few times, but it was not enough. So you visit them in their house, with the presence of her *maḥram*. It is not permissible for a man and a woman who are not lawful for each other to be physically present in the same place. It is important to avoid being alone together in private. It is not permissible for them to be behind closed doors together, as *shayṭan* becomes the third presence in such situations. By keeping the door open and maintaining an open environment, we can freely engage in conversations while ensuring appropriate boundaries. In order to ensure clarity and alignment, recording and writing down the discussions can be beneficial. It is crucial to remember that this is about marriage, not a casual relationship between boyfriend and girlfriend. We should take into consideration the guidance of the Prophet (s.w.t.) regarding this matter, as it holds significance for both brothers and sisters. This is so beautiful, he (s.a.w.) says:

مِنْ سَعَادَةِ ابْنِ آدَمَ رِضَاهُ بِمَا قَضَى اللَّهُ لَهُ وَمِنْ شَقَاوَةِ ابْنِ آدَمَ تَرْكُهُ اسْتِخَارَةَ اللَّهِ وَمِنْ شَقَاوَةِ ابْنِ آدَمَ سَخَطُهُ بِمَا قَضَى اللَّهُ لَهُ.

From (the signs of) the son of Adam's prosperity, is his satisfaction with what Allah decreed for him, and from the son of Adam's misery is his avoiding to request guidance from Allah, and from the son of Adam's misery is his anger with what Allah decreed for him.

Jami' at-Tirmidhi 2151

True happiness in any decision comes from consulting Allah (s.w.t.). Do you believe that Allah would deceive you? Or that Allah would not guide you towards what is best after seeking His guidance? This is particularly relevant when you are uncertain and undecided. However, if you have already made a decision, such as booking a wedding hall and paying for the arrangements in full, and then later deciding to pray *istikharah*, its effectiveness may be diminished. You might mistakenly feel a sense of assurance and say, "*Alḥamdulillāh*, I feel very good about it." In reality, you do not truly feel good about it because you have already made the decision beforehand. It is similar to when you go to sleep after eagerly anticipating something, like a field trip when you were young. Let's say the destination was Disney, Niagara Falls, or any exciting place. As kids, our dreams would be filled with images of that upcoming field trip. Therefore, it is not merely a dream but a reflection of what we have been constantly thinking about and deeply absorbed in. Therefore, it is important to clarify that you cannot finalise all decisions and then pray *istikharah*. *Istikharah* should be performed when you are genuinely undecided and seeking Allah's (s.w.t.) choice for you with utmost sincerity and honesty. A clear indication of a person's misery is when they choose to avoid seeking guidance from Allah (s.w.t.). Furthermore, even after requesting guidance from Allah and being shown multiple signs indicating a negative outcome, persisting in pursuing that course of action leads to further distress and unhappiness.

Engagement

What is engagement? The concept of engagement in Islam is a simple promise to get married in the future, without any implied permissions or allowances. It does not change the status of what is halal or haram. For example, being engaged does not make going out together, being alone, shaking hands, hugging, or exchanging kisses permissible. These actions remain prohibited, as they would be between any unrelated man and woman. It is important to understand that engagement does not establish a legal relationship that permits such interactions.

During my visit to New York City, I encountered a man accompanied by three children and a woman in a shop. The man was purchasing a wedding suit for himself and matching suits for his children, who were of different ages. Curiosity led us to engage in conversation, and I assumed that their mother had passed away and he was remarrying. However, he clarified that she was actually the mother of the children, and they had been together for 11 years. They recently realised their love for each other and decided that it was finally time to formalise their relationship through marriage. *Mashā'Allāh*. In Islam, touching the hand of a woman who is not lawful for you is considered haram. Furthermore, actions such as hugging, kissing, and seeing a woman without a hijab are also prohibited. Dating, as commonly understood in modern contexts, is not permissible within the framework of Islamic teachings. I am here to provide information about what is considered halal and haram according to Islamic principles. Ultimately, the choice to follow a particular path is up to each individual.

In Islam, engagement is understood as a simple promise to marry. It does not require any formal contracts, written agreements, witnesses, or specific procedures. There is no obligation to throw a party or follow certain rituals. Engagement occurs when a man proposes to a woman, and the family accepts the proposal, expressing their happiness and acceptance of the prospective son-in-law. This creates a condition of *khitbah* or engagement.

However, it is important to note that engagement is not a binding commitment, and either party can call it off without any legal consequences. The only commitment that may arise during engagement is if the fiancé has given valuable gifts to the fiancée, such as a Rolex watch, diamond ring, or luxury purse. In such cases, it is expected to return those gifts if the engagement is called off, unless the fiancé insists that the fiancée keeps them. These gifts are given to impress the potential spouse and do not serve as a formal *mahr* (dowry).

Engagement is essentially a promise to marry, and it is essential to understand its nature and limitations within Islamic teachings. The Prophet (s.a.w.) said:

> It was narrated from Ibn 'Umar that the Prophet said: "None of you should propose marriage to a woman when someone else has already proposed to her."

> Sunan an-Nasa'i 3238

If you are aware that another Muslim brother has already proposed to the same girl, it is important to step back and respect their engagement. It is not permissible to try to win over the family or attempt to offer more dowry or gifts in an effort to surpass the previous proposal. This behaviour is not in accordance with Islamic principles. However, if the engagement between the girl and the other brother is broken, then it would be acceptable to proceed with your own proposal. It is crucial to uphold integrity and respect the commitments made in engagements between other individuals.

ʿIddah

It is not permissible to propose to a divorced woman or a widow during their *ʿiddah* period. The *ʿiddah* is a waiting period prescribed by Allah (s.w.t.) and mentioned in the Qur'an, specifically in Surah At-Ṭalaq. The *ʿiddah* serves as a period of reflection, adjustment, and mourning for the woman who has undergone a divorce or lost her husband through death. During this time, she is not allowed to enter into a new marriage contract or accept marriage proposals. It is essential to respect the *ʿiddah* period and give the woman the necessary time and space to complete this waiting period before considering any proposals.

... ٱلنَّبِىُّ إِذَا طَلَّقْتُمُ ٱلنِّسَآءَ فَطَلِّقُوهُنَّ لِعِدَّتِهِـنَّ وَأَحْصُـوا ٱلْعِـدَّةَ ۖ ...

…when you [Muslims] divorce women, divorce them for [the commencement of] their waiting period and keep count of the waiting period,…

(aṭ-Ṭalaq:1)

It is true that divorce can occur in marriages, and even the Prophet Muhammad (s.a.w.) divorced some of his wives during his lifetime. After the first and second divorces, there is a waiting period called *'iddah*. This waiting period is typically three menstrual cycles or three periods of purification following menstruation. However, if a woman does not experience menstruation due to menopause or other reasons, the waiting period is three lunar months.

It is important to note that during the *'iddah* period, the woman is still considered married. The waiting period provides a time of reflection, reconciliation, and potential reconciliation between the husband and wife. If the couple decides to reconcile and continue their marriage during this period, they can do so without the need for a new marriage contract.

$$\text{وَٱلَّذِينَ يُتَوَفَّوْنَ مِنكُمْ وَيَذَرُونَ أَزْوَٰجًا يَتَرَبَّصْنَ بِأَنفُسِهِنَّ أَرْبَعَةَ أَشْهُرٍ وَعَشْرًا ...}$$

And those who are taken in death among you and leave wives behind - they, [the wives, shall] wait four months and ten [days]...

(al-Baqarah:234)

The waiting period for a widow is four months and ten days. During this time, it is not permissible for anyone to propose to her out of respect for the deceased husband. This period allows the widow to grieve and adjust to her loss. It is important to honour this time and refrain from making any marriage proposals.

Similarly, if a woman is in the *ʿiddah* period following divorce, it is strictly forbidden to propose to her or engage in any discussions regarding marriage. During the *ʿiddah*, the woman is still considered married to her former husband, and any attempts to propose or pursue a relationship with her are not permissible.

In both cases, whether it is the *ʿiddah* of divorce or the iddah of death, it is crucial to uphold the Islamic teachings and refrain from engaging in any actions that disrespect the sanctity of marriage and the waiting period. The mentioned verse from Surah al-Baqarah verse 235 emphasises the prohibition of proposing to a woman who has lost her husband during the *ʿiddah* period. Allah (s.w.t.) said:

وَلَا جُنَاحَ عَلَيْكُمْ فِيمَا عَرَّضْتُم بِهِ مِنْ خِطْبَةِ النِّسَآءِ أَوْ أَكْنَنتُمْ فِيٓ أَنفُسِكُمْ ۚ ...

There is no blame upon you for that to which you [indirectly] allude concerning a proposal to women or for what you conceal within yourselves...

In the case of a widow, it is considered impermissible to directly propose marriage to her during the *ʿiddah* period. However, it is not forbidden to give a subtle hint or offer words of encouragement, especially when the widow is facing difficulties and feeling distressed. For instance, if someone tells her, "Don't worry sister, many people will be interested in you," implying their own interest in marriage. However, it is important to note that making a direct proposal and saying, *"Inshā'Allāh,* I will marry you after the *ʿiddah,"* is considered forbidden out of respect for the previous marital bond between the widow and her deceased husband. This understanding is derived from the meaning of the mentioned verse.

Nikaḥ

The term *nikaḥ* is mentioned several times in the Qur'an and it carries two distinct meanings. The first meaning refers to the marriage contract itself, as mentioned in Surah al-Baqarah, verse 235:

$$\text{...وَلَا تَعْزِمُوا۟ عُقْدَةَ ٱلنِّكَاحِ}$$

And do not determine to undertake a marriage contract (nikaḥ)...

The second meaning of *nikaḥ* refers to sexual contact or the consummation of the marriage, also known as *dukhul*. This occurs when a husband and wife are alone behind closed doors, even if they do not engage in sexual relations. The act of being alone together, with the opportunity for physical intimacy, constitutes *dukhul*.

From the Islamic perspective, if a marriage contract has been established and the couple moves in together, even if they have not engaged in sexual relations, the woman is entitled to all the rights and obligations associated with marriage. This includes the full dowry (*mahr*) and the waiting period (*'iddah*) in the case of divorce. The actual consummation of the marriage is not the determining factor; rather, the opportunity for intimacy behind closed doors is considered sufficient for the act of *dukhul* or consummation.

Therefore, *nikah* encompasses both the marriage contract (*'uqdatan nikah*) and the potential for sexual relations or the consummation of the marriage.

In Surah an-Nur verse 32, Allah (s.w.t.) uses the word *nikah* to refer to a marriage contract:

$$\text{وَأَنكِحُوا۟ ٱلْأَيَـٰمَىٰ مِنكُمْ وَٱلصَّـٰلِحِينَ مِنْ عِبَادِكُمْ وَإِمَآئِكُمْ...}$$

And marry the unmarried among you and the righteous among your male slaves and female slaves...

(an-Nur:32)

Allah (s.w.t.) commands us to marry those who are single among men and women and to help them in their pursuit of marriage. This commandment emphasises the importance of facilitating the marriage process and supporting individuals in finding suitable partners.

When it comes to the marriage contract, it must fulfill certain pillars and conditions. It is crucial to understand the requirements and rulings related to marriage, not just limited to one specific school of thought or legal opinion. For example, a person might only be aware of a particular ruling within the Hanafi school of thought that allows a girl to marry without the consent of her guardian. However, it is essential to have a comprehensive understanding of the rulings and perspectives of different scholars and schools of thought before making any decisions related to marriage.

In order for a marriage to be valid, certain pillars and conditions must be fulfilled. One of the important pillars is that the groom and bride must be free of legal impediments, such as being *mahram* to each other. Being *mahram* means having a close familial relationship that prohibits marriage.

For example, if someone asks whether their cousin is considered *mahram* to them, the answer is no. Cousins are not considered *mahram* to each other, which means they are not prohibited from marrying each other. So, it is permissible for individuals to marry their cousins if they choose to do so. As an example, Prophet Muhammad (s.a.w.) married his cousin, Zaynab bint Jahsh (r.a.). This serves as an example that marrying one's cousin is permissible in Islam.

The establishment of a *maḥram* relationship can occur through fostering, breastfeeding, or suckling. If a nursing woman who has a baby daughter breastfeeds a baby boy who is not related to her at least five fulfilling times, they are considered *maḥram* to each other, treating them as siblings. As a result, they are prohibited from marrying each other.

The concept of *maḥram* is mentioned in Surah an-Nisa'verse 23. This verse outlines the individuals who are considered *maḥram*, with whom marriage is forbidden due to close family ties and relationships. The purpose of these regulations is to maintain appropriate boundaries and prevent potential instances of incestuous relationships.

حُرِّمَتْ عَلَيْكُمْ أُمَّهَـٰتُكُمْ وَبَنَاتُكُمْ وَأَخَوَٰتُكُمْ وَعَمَّـٰتُكُمْ وَخَـٰلَـٰتُكُمْ وَبَنَاتُ ٱلْأَخِ وَبَنَاتُ ٱلْأُخْـتِ وَأُمَّهَـٰتُكُمُ ٱلَّـٰتِىٓ أَرْضَعْنَكُمْ وَأَخَوَٰتُكُم مِّنَ ٱلرَّضَـٰعَةِ وَأُمَّهَـٰتُ نِسَآئِكُمْ وَرَبَـٰٓئِبُكُمُ ٱلَّـٰتِى فِى حُجُورِكُم مِّن نِّسَآئِكُمُ ٱلَّـٰتِى دَخَلْتُم بِهِنَّ فَإِن لَّمْ تَكُونُوا۟ دَخَلْتُم بِهِنَّ فَلَا جُنَاحَ عَلَيْكُمْ وَحَلَـٰٓئِلُ أَبْنَآئِكُمُ ٱلَّذِينَ مِنْ أَصْلَـٰبِكُمْ وَأَن تَجْمَعُوا۟ بَيْنَ ٱلْأُخْتَيْنِ إِلَّا مَا قَدْ سَلَفَ ۗ إِنَّ ٱللَّهَ كَانَ غَفُورًا رَّحِيمًا ۝٢٣

Prohibited to you [for marriage] are your mothers, your daughters, your sisters, your father's sisters, your mother's sisters, your brother's daughters, your sister's daughters, your [milk] mothers who nursed you, your sisters through nursing, your wives' mothers, and your step-daughters under your guardianship [born] of your wives unto whom you have gone in. But if you have not gone in unto them, there is no sin upon you. And [also prohibited are] the wives of your sons who are from your [own] loins, and that you take [in marriage] two sisters simultaneously, except for what has already occurred. Indeed, Allah is ever Forgiving and Merciful.

(an-Nisa':23)

Those are the women who are your *mahram*. You can never marry them. Europe is now opening to legalise family incest and make it even legal to marry constitutionally. May Allah (s.w.t.) protect us. You know the world is living in filth. May Allah guide us to what is best.

The second pillar is the consent of the guardian. Any marriage without the consent of the guardian is invalid. The Prophet (s.a.w.) said so an *ijab* and *qabul* which is a proposal and an agreement or acceptance. So in the case of a man, Allah (s.w.t.) says in Surah al-Maidah verse 5:

...And [lawful in marriage are] chaste women from among the believers and chaste women from among those who were given the Scripture before you, when you have given them their due compensation, desiring chastity, not unlawful sexual intercourse or taking [secret] lovers...

(al-Maidah:5)

In Islam, the condition of *ihsan* refers to the requirement of chastity or moral integrity when considering marriage. It is important to seek a spouse who maintains a virtuous and chaste lifestyle. Engaging in a relationship with someone who is not chaste, such as a person who has just ended a relationship, is discouraged in Islam.

Regarding interfaith marriages, Muslim women are generally not allowed to marry non-Muslim men according to the majority view in Islamic jurisprudence. The purpose behind this restriction is to ensure the preservation of faith and to avoid potential conflicts in matters of religious practice and upbringing of children.

We all know that there is an *'iddah* for a woman. Have you ever heard of an *'iddah* for a man? If a man is married to four women and he divorced one of them in order to marry another woman, he cannot marry her right away. Why? Because if he divorces one of his wives, they are still officially married until the *'iddah* is over. So he has to wait for the *'iddah* of the wife whom he divorced, so she is not his wife anymore, in order to marry another one. That is the only condition.

In addition to the pillars of marriage, there are certain conditions that must be fulfilled for a marriage to be valid. These conditions include the mutual consent and approval of the couple, known as *ijab* and *qabul*. If a woman offers herself in marriage to a man and he does not agree or accept, the marriage cannot take place. It is customary for the guardian to play a role in facilitating the marriage and their consent is required for the marriage to be valid, along with the presence of witnesses.

The Prophet (s.a.w.) said in a sound hadith which is narrated by 'A'ishah (r.a.):

The Messenger of Allah said:

"Whichever woman married without the permission of her waliyy her marriage is invalid, her marriage is invalid, her marriage is invalid. If he entered into her, then the Mahr is for her in lieu of what he enjoyed from her private part. If they disagree, then the Sultan is the waliyy for one who has no waliyy."

Jami' at-Tirmidhi 1102

So, a girl who marries without the consent of her guardian essentially means that she is not married. This relationship is considered illegal and serves as a lesson. However, Shaykh, have you ever encountered a situation where many people propose to me, but my guardian keeps refusing? For instance, one hundred people have proposed to me, yet he continues to decline. Why does this happen? Well, he wants me to marry his nephew, cousin, or the son of his friend. In such cases, if we discover that the guardian, even if he is the father himself, is rejecting proposals without a legitimate reason, his guardianship is not guaranteed. It will be taken away from him and given to the next in line. If the grandfather is alive, he will have the right to guardianship; otherwise, it will pass to the uncle or, if the brothers are grown up, to them. Nonetheless, a woman cannot give herself in marriage without the presence of a guardian.

Now, what about revert sisters who do not have any Muslim family members? In some countries, the Sultan or those in charge of Muslim societies can act as the guardian and be happy to facilitate the process. However, in America, where we do not have such a system, the imam of the mosque may serve as the guardian. Can I simply go to the imam and request him to be my guardian? Yes, you can. However, granting guardianship is not just a matter of words. If the imam agrees to be your guardian, it means that he will also protect your rights, help you overcome any problems, investigate matters, and act as your representative in case of future disputes or even divorce. Guardianship is not a mere formality; it carries significant responsibilities.

Additionally, at least two Muslim witnesses are required during the marriage contract. But when we say 'just witnesses', what does it mean in practice in Islam? It means that the witnesses should be individuals known for their adherence to Islam. For example, a person who is known to consume alcohol would not be accepted as a witness, and the same goes for someone who rarely prays or only offers prayers inconsistently. Such individuals would be considered rebellious, and their testimony would not be accepted.

Now, can anyone be a guardian? No, simply being the father does not automatically make him the guardian. If a girl accepts Islam and her father is not fit to be her guardian—her guardian must be a Muslim, an adult, and of good character. Furthermore, the guardian must be male; a mother cannot fulfill this role. Therefore, a wife is not sufficient to make the right decisions on behalf of the girl under her guardianship. When we contemplate this, we realise that all of these regulations are in place for the benefit of the girl. She does not have to demand her rights; her guardian will do so on her behalf. She does not have to go out and investigate the background of the person proposing to her, his family, his work, income, or history; her guardian will handle all of that. Moreover, in case of conflicts or disputes, the guardian will represent her to ensure her rights are protected. The guardian is the best person to understand and know the girl under his guardianship.

Mahr

The dowry holds a special status in marriage. It is neither a pillar nor a condition for the validity of the marriage, but rather it is considered *wajib*. There is a significant difference between a pillar and something obligatory. If a woman marries without the consent of her guardian, the entire marriage contract is invalid as it did not take place. There were no witnesses, and if the man marrying a Muslim girl is not Muslim, the pillars of the marriage contract are not fulfilled. Similarly, if these issues are rectified, the marriage contract must be redone.

However, in a case where a girl was excited and her guardian was pleased with a proposal, and they got married without specifying the dowry, is the marriage contract invalid? No, it is not. The dowry can still be determined and agreed upon after the marriage contract. Therefore, the dowry is compulsory, but it can be paid after the marriage contract, whether a specific dowry amount was agreed upon or not. In case of a dispute, one can look into the dowries of sisters, cousins, or girls of similar circumstances to determine an appropriate amount.

The dowry does not have to be paid upfront or in full immediately. It can be deferred, either partially or entirely. Furthermore, the dowry does not have to be in the form of cash, gold, or silver; it can also include services or knowledge that the husband will provide, as mentioned in Surah an-Nisa' in the Qur'an.

It is important to note that the dowry belongs to the wife, and it is not permissible for anyone, including the guardian (even if the guardian is the father), to take any part of it. Some parents may consider the dowry as their right and take it for themselves when the girl marries. However, this is not permissible. The dowry is the wife's property, and she has the right to dispense it as she pleases. If she wishes to give part of it to her husband, and parents, or donate it entirely to charity, it is entirely her decision. No one, including the guardian, has the right to claim any part of it without her consent. However, if the wife willingly decides to forgo or give a part of the dowry to her husband, it is permissible for him to accept it.

With regards to the nature of the dowry and it does not have to be money. The Prophet (s.a.w.) mentioned in a hadith:

Sahl bin Sa'd said:

"I was among the people with the Prophet when a woman stood up and said: 'O' Messenger of Allah, she has offered herself in marriage to you, so see what you think of her.' He remained silent and the Prophet did not give any answer. Then she stood up (again) and said: 'O' Messenger of Allah, she has offered herself in marriage to you, so see what you think of her.' A man stood up and said: 'Marry her to me, O' Messenger of Allah!' He said: 'Do you have anything?' He said: 'No.' He said: 'Go and look, even if it is just an iron ring.' So he went and looked then he came and said: 'I could not find anything, not even an iron ring.' He said: 'Have you memorised anything of the Qur'an?' He said: 'Yes, Surah such-and-such and Surah such-and-such.' He said: 'I will marry you to her on the basis of what you have memorized of the Qur'an.'"

Sunan an-Nasa'i 3280

Indeed, the dowry can take various forms and can include services or benefits that the husband provides to the wife. An example of this can be found in the story of Musa (a.s.) mentioned in Surah al-Qaṣaṣ verse 27, where the father of the two girls offered Musa (a.s.) one of his daughters in marriage in exchange for his help and labour for a certain period of time. Musa (a.s.) agreed, and the service he provided became the dowry for his wife.

It is worth noting that it is highly recommended to be moderate and reasonable when it comes to wedding gifts, dowry, and other related expenses. Islam encourages moderation in all matters, including marriage, and emphasises the importance of not burdening oneself or others with excessive demands or financial obligations. The focus should be on the sincerity and compatibility of the marriage rather than material possessions or extravagant demands.

To the extent that the Prophet (a.s.) said in one hadith:

The woman who brings the greatest blessing is the one whose wedding arrangements are the most moderate.

(Musnad Aḥmad, 24595)

Indeed, it is important to maintain moderation and affordability when it comes to wedding expenses and dowry. Excessive demands and high expectations can create financial burdens that many young people are unable to bear. This issue is particularly prevalent in certain regions where extravagant weddings and large dowries are considered the norm.

The Prophet Muhammad (s.a.w.) advised us to keep marriage simple and affordable. He (s.a.w.) emphasised the blessings in a marriage that is within one's means and does not burden the couple or their families. It is unfortunate that these excessive demands often result in many young individuals, especially women, remaining unmarried for prolonged periods or even for their entire lives.

Islam encourages us to prioritise the sincerity, compatibility, and well-being of the couple over material possessions and extravagant displays. It is important to remember that the essence of marriage lies in the love, understanding, and commitment between the husband and wife, rather than the lavishness of the wedding or the dowry. By adhering to the teachings of moderation and affordability, we can create a more inclusive and accessible environment for marriage, ensuring that more individuals have the opportunity to enter into this blessed institution.

Regarding the issue of deferred dowry, it is important to clarify its nature and misconception. Many people mistakenly believe that the deferred dowry is only payable in the event of divorce. However, this understanding is incorrect. When the dowry is deferred, it means that it is a loan from the wife to the husband, and it should be settled once the husband has the means to do so.

In Islamic inheritance laws, before dividing the deceased's inheritance, any outstanding debts must be settled, including the deferred dowry. If the husband passes away, his debts, including the deferred dowry, should be paid off before distributing the inheritance to the heirs. Even if the entire inheritance is required to settle the debt, it is necessary to fulfill the husband's financial obligations.

It is crucial to understand that the deferred dowry is not tied to divorce or death specifically. If a husband promises a certain amount as a dowry but is currently unable to pay due to financial constraints, it becomes a debt that he owes to his wife. Once his financial situation improves, he should settle the deferred dowry without delay.

It is recommended for husbands to fulfill their financial responsibilities and settle any outstanding debts, including the deferred dowry, as soon as they are able to do so. By fulfilling these obligations, they uphold their integrity and honour the rights of their wives.

Walimah

Regarding the recommendation to announce a marriage, it is highly encouraged in Islam. The Prophet Muhammad (s.a.w.) advised believers to publicise their marriages, making it known to the community. This practice helps avoid misunderstandings and ensures transparency in marital relationships.

When a marriage is announced, it serves as a way to inform others that a person is now married and should be regarded as such. This prevents any assumptions or misconceptions about the relationship between individuals of the opposite gender. By openly announcing the marriage, people are aware of the commitment and bond between the couple.

There are instances from the time of the Prophet Muhammad (s.a.w.) where he himself advised his companions to announce their marriages. For example, when one of his companions, Sa'd ibn Abi Waqqas, married a woman named Safiyyah, the Prophet instructed him to inform others about the marriage. This was to ensure that there were no doubts or suspicions surrounding their relationship.

The purpose of announcing a marriage is to safeguard one's reputation and maintain a clear and respectful image within the community. By making the marriage known, it helps prevent any misunderstandings, inappropriate advances, or proposals from others who may be unaware of the person's marital status.

Announcing a marriage does not simply mean sharing the news verbally. It can also involve celebrating and rejoicing in a manner that is permissible in Islam, such as gathering with family and friends, expressing happiness, and exchanging congratulations. It is important to observe the principles of modesty and avoid any excessive or extravagant practices.

The *walimah* is also an emphatic sunnah, meaning it is highly recommended in Islam. It refers to a wedding feast or banquet that is traditionally hosted by the husband after the marriage ceremony. The purpose of the *walimah* is to express gratitude to Allah (s.w.t.) for facilitating the marriage and to seek blessings for the newlywed couple.

The *walimah* is an opportunity to gather family, friends, and community members to celebrate the marriage. By inviting guests and hosting them, the couple seeks blessings and well-wishes from those in attendance. When people attend the *walimah* and pray for the couple's happiness and success, it is considered beneficial for them.

It is important to note that the *walimah* should not be a display of extravagance or a means of showing off wealth. Instead, it should be a humble and moderate gathering within the means of the couple. It is not necessary to go into debt or spend excessively to host a lavish *walimah*. The focus should be on gratitude, thanksgiving, and sharing blessings with others.

In terms of the food served at the *walimah*, it should be whatever the couple can afford. There is no specific requirement for the type or quality of food. It can be simple and modest, such as offering basic dishes and serving guests with generosity and hospitality. The emphasis is on gathering people together, sharing a meal, and fostering a sense of community.

Examples from the time of the Prophet Muhammad (s.a.w.) demonstrate that the *walimah* can be conducted in a humble manner. For instance, the Prophet provided a *walimah* with meat and bread on the occasion of his marriage to Zaynab bint Jahsh, and on another occasion, he offered a *walimah* with barley remains.

It is worth mentioning that attending the *walimah* is considered a communal duty for those who receive an invitation. However, if someone is unable to attend due to valid reasons, such as being out of town or having prior commitments, they are not held blameworthy. Attending the *walimah* is encouraged as it strengthens community bonds and supports the couple in their new journey of marriage.

In conclusion, the *walimah* is a recommended practice in Islam that signifies gratitude, blessings, and community celebration. It should be conducted with moderation, within one's means, and with a focus on expressing thanks to Allah and sharing joy with others.

Q&A

Q1: My husband is having a relationship with someone else's wife. I have been very ṣabr for many years. He knows that I know about it. And we have spoken about it too, but he still ignores my feelings. What should I do?

A: May Allah (s.w.t.) guide him. Doing the sin is something and doing it while not feeling remorse upon doing it is something else. A person who's caught doing something like that should be regretful, fearful, and remorseful, apologise and make promises that he will not do it again. A person who is insisting on doing it and ignores it is he, right? Right. And he ignores his wife, and her rights and is indeed a sinner. By the way, we do not know either one of them. The question is from an anonymous person, so this is not a judgment. This is *fatwa*. And there is a huge difference between the *fatwa* and the *ḥukum* and the judgment. OK, maybe the wife would go to her house and say what the Shaykh today said about you. You're a big sinner, I didn't. I don't know who he is. Well, I'm talking about the act itself. If somebody is blessed with a good wife, he should appreciate this *ni'mah*. And guess what? If the wife knows that the husband is involved in an illicit relationship, and he is now planning to quit. She is entitled to ask for a divorce and get rid of him. This means that she should give him the ultimatum. She doesn't have to accept this kind of life and may Allah (s.w.t.) guide him. And if they have children? You should understand that that would have a severe negative impact on their children. *Subḥānallāh*, how can a person? Not think that what about if the other spouse would do the same thing? Would you accept it? It would be shameful. Likewise, you should be ashamed of yourself. You should fear, remorse, regret, seek forgiveness and quit immediately.

Q2: I have a friend and she's against getting married. Due to the condition of marriages nowadays like divorces and cheating and so on. I've tried convincing her multiple times but she's against it. So can you give us advice?

A: Well, unfortunately, sometimes a person may get paranoid. You know, up until this moment, there are people still not only wearing masks that are afraid to shake hands, they are afraid to touch things since COVID-19. So as a result of that, their life has been affected by a great deal. He or she needs counselling. Around you, there are thousands of cases who are happily married. Having beautiful kids, you know, you don't know what you're missing. Well, like you don't know what you're missing, I'm not talking only about the sexual relations. I'm talking about having a child. Imagine growing old with them. Then losing the chance to have a child, then you wake up—too late. Too late. It was all your fault. You know the most beautiful thing in life is to have a child to play with, to teach him or her to do things, to play, to pray, to read Qur'an, to go to school. So you're wasting this opportunity and it is a limited time offer. It is not for good. So take advantage, and convey the message to her. She needs counselling. You definitely need counselling and to take advantage of this opportunity before it is too late. Look around you. *Alḥamdulillāh*, not every couple is divorced. If you make the right decision from the beginning inshā'Allāh, Allah will bless you with a good spouse and a goodly offspring. Do we know the unseen? No, we don't. Somebody is having phobia against planes, so he doesn't even go for *ʿumrah* or *ḥajj*. Because 20 years ago a plane crashed. But there are millions of other flights dropping people right and left from point A to point B with safety. So you do not just anticipate the same will happen to you and accordingly, you suspend your entire life. May Allah make it easy for her.

Q3: My question, my question is not related to this topic, but it's related to the new age movement or religious science which is famous in us. So this is related to law of attraction, affirmation, power for energy, power of imagination. I don't care about those non-Muslims but this affecting Muslim nowadays and some of it like relates it to Islam. So your opinion on this?

A: We are all familiar with feminism. But there is something worse nowadays, which is Muslim feminists. When it was the ayat and ahadith and bring feminism into Islam. They do not work together. Allah (s.w.t.) already established the *huquq* of the woman and the *wajibat* of a woman. Likewise, a *huquq* of a man and the *wajibat* of a man. In Surah an-Nisa' there is an ayah that says it's either you choose to be a believer, or you don't want to. And it is actions speak louder than words. It is not by theories; it is by practice. I mean in the States for instance, in the West, when a woman is divorced, she is entitled to have half of the wealth of the husband. Not Muslim women do that all the time in order to take half the wealth of the men. If a Muslim woman have this chance, would it be permissible for her to take half of his wealth? She is not permitted to do so. All because we live in America. And this is my right, your right is what Allah (s.w.t.) stated for you. More than that, that's called transgression. Islam is whole and inseparable. You either take it all or you leave it all. You don't pick and choose to be a true Muslim woman. Nothing is hidden. Everything is explained in detail. Likewise with a man to be a practising Muslim man or a good husband or a righteous husband. Everything is explained in the guidance of the Prophet (s.a.w.). When you do otherwise, you're not a true husband, you're not a true Muslim.

Q4: If marriage is half of completing my *deen*, can a woman who's never got the *rizq* to get married till old age gets to complete half of her *deen*? If there is a way, in what ways?

A: There is always a way as long as there is a will and there is no age limit. There is no age limit. You know, and instead of spending the rest of your life by yourself and the remaining part of your life, especially when you grow old and you are lonely, it's really bad. The best part of your life is when you reach an old age with your spouse. Or, in case the spouse dies, then you have children to look after you and to socialise with, and so on. Allah (s.w.t.) doesn't prescribe or commend anything but for great wisdom. So *Alḥamdulillāh*, if you realise right now that I should fulfill half of my *deen*. And by the way, we spoke about the marriage undergoing the five legal *aḥkam*. So not for everyone marriage is *wajib* or marriage is recommended. Some people—Ibn Taymiyyah never got married. He devoted his life to learning and teaching and giving *da'wah*. He was not interested. Is it haram? No. So in your case, *Alḥamdulillāh wa shukrillāh* if you have a chance to get married at any age, *Bismillāh*. And if you do it with this intention to complete half of your *deen*, then *inshā'Allāh* you will receive the reward equivalent to that.

Q5: I watched several lectures before saying if we repeatedly declined marriage proposals, Allah might not send us anyone any longer in the future. So sometimes this fills me with fear and hopelessness. Is this any way true?

A: This is not exactly true. And it may be true in one condition. The first segment of my answer. This is not exactly true—if all the proposals are terrible. You don't have to accept any form. Some proposals I would rather live as single and not marry this guy. You're not blameworthy for not accepting this proposal. But the hadith says: "When someone with whose religion and character you are satisfied asks your daughter in marriage, accede to his request." If *Mashā'Allāh*, Allah blesses you with the right and decent person. Any girl would like him. But you're thinking about Tom Cruise or waiting for Tom Cruise. You'll be waiting forever. So when will you be considered blameworthy? When everyone around you tells you. This guy is not to be missed. This proposal is not to be wasted. Look, *Mashā'Allāh*, he is a complete package, so this is an eye-opener. And that's why we said before you praised *istikharah*, there is *mashurah*. You know your guardian will be doing the investigation and consulting his neighbours. And you will be consulting your peer. The girls around you, what do you think of him? He's cute. This is a good opportunity. So it's an eye-opener for you. But to say generally that Allah will punish you because you refused 3 or 4 proposals? What if all of them were terrible?

Q6: Is there *du'a'* to open my heart to not be afraid of man and marriage?

A: Oh, yes, yes, yes, there, there is a beautiful *du'a':*

$$وَٱلَّذِينَ يَقُولُونَ رَبَّنَا هَبْ لَنَا مِنْ أَزْوَٰجِنَا وَذُرِّيَّـٰتِنَا قُرَّةَ أَعْيُنٍ وَٱجْعَلْنَا لِلْمُتَّقِينَ إِمَامًا ٧٤$$

And those who say, "Our Lord, grant us from among our wives and offspring comfort to our eyes and make us a leader [i.e., example] for the righteous."

(al-Furqan:74)

Do you think this *du'a'* is only meant to be recited by a married couple? No. Whether you are married or you're single, you're asking Allah to bless you with a spouse who will be the comfort for your eyes, peace for your mind, and with goodly offspring. And the second one *du'a'* is:

$$وَمِنْهُم مَّن يَقُولُ رَبَّنَا ءَاتِنَا فِى ٱلدُّنْيَا حَسَنَةً وَفِى ٱلْءَاخِرَةِ حَسَنَةً وَقِنَا عَذَابَ ٱلنَّارِ ٢٠١$$

But among them is he who says, "Our Lord, give us in this world [that which is] good and in the Hereafter [that which is] good and protect us from the punishment of the Fire."

(al-Baqarah:201)

These two supplications supplicate to Allah with the intention of seeking the best spouse.

Q7: I have this one friend who likes the same gender as himself. So how do I advise him as a friend?

A: I have some cases where people telling me: "I don't feel attracted to women. Rather, I feel attracted to men." And he's a man. Let me break it down to you, so we exactly know what we're talking about here. 20 years ago, no one would dare to reveal that they are gay. even in the States, it was perceived as taboo. The US Army, 10 years ago would not accept gays. They will be fired. Even Boy Scouts and Girl Scouts. It is because the world has changed and started more accepting what is haram. It makes it halal. This means that: If you remember when we spoke about love and we said Islam acknowledges love, appreciates love. But we also said one thing unless this love is haram. Can you say, "I love this woman." when she is married? No. "But I love her." No, this is haram. In this case you're supposed to overcome your desire. This is not love. This is haram desire. So whenever there is a haram desire, you're supposed to do *istighfar*, *ta'awudz* and resist. Resist the urge to even think about the haram relationship. Likewise when you know that in Islam there is no such sexual relation between the same gender in Islam. This is called *luat*. This is called *sihab* between the girls and *luat* between the men. It is haram and it is a major sin. How about adultery? Is adultery, halal or haram? Is it because somebody cannot resist the urge of having sexual relations, we say it's OK. What can we do? It's, you know, against his will. If he is attractive, so it's OK to commit adultery. Likewise it is not any different as long as it is not hard halal to commit adultery. Also it is not permissible in Islam to have such sexual relationships with the same gender. It is purely Islamic, 100% a general consensus. You will not find any different opinion. So when any person has an evil thought that crosses their mind as I mentioned earlier. Somebody fantasizes about a woman who's married, that is haram. Mere thinking about it is forbidden, so every time there is an evil thought that crosses your mind, ward it off and say *a'ūdhubillāhiminashshayṭānirrajīm*. Obviously I normally advise such people to have private counselling because there are further procedures and steps to be followed to overcome the haram feeling and thoughts.

Q8: How to spark a relationship between husband and wife? Don't get me wrong, our relationship is super happy. It is always glad to be home with her or him. Sometimes I struggle finding a new way to spark it.

A: Sometimes, due to watching too much drama and Hollywood movies. You feel like you know, my life is not doing good enough and I want to spark our marital relationship and spice it out? Nowadays, most men are crushed at work to earn their living. To provide for the family. People are getting laid off and fired right and left. Economies are being collapsing here and there. Businesses are going sour. So you got to keep in mind that because you have plenty of time in your hands. So that you can watch this and think about that it is not necessarily the same with the man. From the moment that he steps out of the house early morning, he's facing hundreds of challenges. Then it is your role when he returns home to be his beauty queen; to be the most beautiful woman in his eye, why don't you take the initiative? Vacationing, doing something together and it doesn't have to be all sexual. You know when there is a project that you can do together which will melt you together in a melting pot such as we are planning to memorise Surah al-Baqarah together. We heard about the refugees here and there and we are raising funds and we will take the food parcels and distribute them. Any project that we will do together, we will bring us closer to each other. And obviously, once we have children, most likely the sister who presented the question doesn't have children yet. This is because once we have children there is not much time to think about spark in your life. You know, you're barely find time when you wake up early morning to prepare them for school, then fix the food, then prepare them for private tutoring, studying their classes, doing their homework, and even when the husband says honey, you're not going to come to bed? You're already passed out an hour ago. So we got to be realistic. Life is really, really tough. But in the midst, the Prophet (s.a.w.) used to race with 'A'ishah (r.a.). Used to sit and listen to her. The Prophet (s.a.w.) was a great listener. She once narrated a long story. Now it is mentioned in hadith in a beautiful poetry. 'A'ishah (r.a.) was a poet. He doesn't mind sitting and listening. So this is an advice for the man. Sometimes whatever you hear makes no sense. But for her, it's the world. It means the world. Really, *Mashā'Allāh*. You know, even if you're not interested, you have to spare time to do so. Going out together, exercising together. If you know I'm into painting and art and so on. The best time is when I invite my wife just to watch as I'm doing an art project. And she keeps saying that that is the best time ever. So based on your availability and what you both can afford, you come up with something to renew your relationship. And obviously, I'll tell you a sincere advice, which is as long as you're making *du'a'* for you and your spouse, Alḥamdulillāh, that would maintain an excellent relationship. The *qabul* goal I've mentioned earlier and even in your mother tongue, you can supplicate to Allah (s.w.t.) to increase the love. Your love in the heart of your husband and the love of your husband in your heart. The second advice is not my advice. It is from 'Abdullah ibn Mas'ud (r.a.). He is saying I can simply detect when I have committed sin. I see the effect of the sin in the behaviour of my wife. And that's a fact. And he's given an example: When a person does something haram. Beginning with the wife, she's having this attitude. She's giving him that look. He doesn't like her cooking any more. It is the same. She hasn't changed. It is you who have changed. So avoiding sins; believe it or not, one of the greatest means of maintaining the marriage. It makes you really appreciate what you have and thanking Allah (s.w.t.) for it day and night. Then expressing about that by thanking your spouse. Whether you are thanking her or she's thanking you. Not necessarily verbally, but also via your actions, your attitude. You know, and the Prophet (s.a.w.) would not leave home—they have called the *iqamah*—'A'ishah (r.a.) would kiss him and he would kiss his wife, even while fasting. There are a lot of couples who do not remember when their last kiss was. Why? They are drowned in debt. He lost his job. He is moving to another company. With all this trouble, it is hard to think about spark in your life. It is already on fire.

Q9: I have a question about dowry, particularly in Malaysia. So what happens in Malaysia, is that there are two types of payment that men make in order to get married, so first there's the *mas kahwin*, which is the dowry. Usually, it is made compulsory by the State for all the men to pay. Each state has a minimum requirement that they have to give in order to get married. For example, some states it is RM300, for others it might less or more. That's wajib for men to make in order to get married in that particular state. Then there's a second type of payment, which we call it *duit hantaran*, which is usually can reach up to thousands and thousands of ringgits. So that is usually the bigger payment that men make. So that's more like traditional or cultural, as you would say, Malaysia. And then most of the time, or at least, you know, in most of the cases of the people around me, you know, the men make the minimum amount of payment. Just the RM300 and then the big portion of money which is the *duit hantaran* goes to the family specifically the parents. Traditionally, it's like, oh, it's the parents' rights for that money that thousands of ringgit and then, you know, with the wife

you only get whatever the minimum money that husband has given according to the State. This makes me think, OK, what exactly is my right? What exactly is the dowry and what is the balanced amount that Islam has been talking about that the husband is supposed to make the payment to the wife and not the family? So please give your advice.

A:	I believe whenever I was addressing the dowry, I would quote verse 4 of Surah an-Nisa'. It is not permissible even for the husband to take back anything out of the dowry that he paid. After they got married so he says give me back that amount. No, because the dowry is the full possession of the wife. It is not for her parents. It is not for her guardian. It is not for anyone else. It is rather her possession and that's why she decided to dispense it in any legal way, such as to give it to a charity or to buy gold for herself. No one has a say in that behaviour. It is absolutely hers. We all know that Islam is not only in one culture, it is multicultural, but whatever cultural traditions that contradict Islam should be dismissed. And if the cultural traditions coincide the Islamic teachings, then *Alḥamdulillāh*, we honour them, we respect them and we go with them. So whenever a husband pays any amount, whether the legal amount which is RM300, or the dowry which is the actual gift, RM300,000 this is entirely for the bride. Not for anyone else. And she is free to give some of that to her parents, to her mother, to her siblings, to give it all for charity, to keep it for herself. This is 100% her right.

Q10: Are we responsible for our spouse during Judgment Day if one person wants to pursue righteousness while the other not so interested?

A: In the Hadith, the Prophet (s.a.w.) said,

> Every one of you is a guardian, and every guardian will be held accountable and questioned by Allah on the day of judgement with regards to those who are under his guardianship.
>
> Mishkat al-Maṣabiḥ 3685

As a husband and a father, my wife is my responsibility. My kids are my responsibility. So if one's wife is wearing those tight jeans and the low-cut shirt or T-shirt and show in the navel, and she's *Mashā'Allāh*, she's not practising and she goes out from his house like that. Is he responsible? 100%. He is responsible, likewise for his children, daughters and sons. But there are things which he has no control over—the private sins, the true relationship with Allah (s.w.t.), as long as my partner *Alḥamdulillāh* prays in front of me and is practising the deen, not disobeying Allah publicly, then you don't know about it. But if you come to know a wife who comes to know that her husband is a drug dealer. And says what can I do? I'm praying for him. Praying is not enough. You need to kick him out. You need to leave him immediately. It is not sufficient to say, "What can I do?" Prayer isn't enough. You have to give him the ultimatum. A husband who is an alcoholic. Why do you keep relations with him if he is not planning to quit? You quit your relationship with him. In Surah al-Muddaththir verse 38 Allah (s.w.t.) said:

$$كُلُّ نَفْسٍ بِمَا كَسَبَتْ رَهِينَةٌ ﴿٣٨﴾$$

Every soul, for what it has earned, will be retained.

Every person will be held accountable for what he or she does. But if I am in a charge of anything or any person under my guardianship, then I would be also liable. In Surah at-Taḥrim verse 6 Allah (s.w.t.) said:

$$يَـٰٓأَيُّهَا ٱلَّذِينَ ءَامَنُوا۟ قُوٓا۟ أَنفُسَكُمْ وَأَهْلِيكُمْ نَارًا وَقُودُهَا ٱلنَّاسُ وَٱلْحِجَارَةُ عَلَيْهَا مَلَـٰٓئِكَةٌ غِلَاظٌ شِدَادٌ لَّا يَعْصُونَ ٱللَّهَ مَآ أَمَرَهُمْ وَيَفْعَلُونَ مَا يُؤْمَرُونَ ﴿٦﴾$$

O' you who have believed, protect yourselves and your families from a Fire whose fuel is people and stones, over which are [appointed] angels, harsh and severe; they do not disobey Allah in what He commands them but do what they are commanded.

Allah (s.w.t.) is addressing the believers: You should protect yourselves and your family members against hell fire not only yourselves. Your son doesn't pray. Why not? He never taught him how to pray. You are blame-worthy. You are liable. Once, I was coming all the way from the States to do *umrah*. The cab driver is a local person. "Where are you from?" He said, "I'm from Makkah. Born and raised there." So I said, "*Mashā'Allāh*, I envy you. I wish I was born and raised in Makkah." He said, "Where you come from? I said I come from the States, he said, "You're the lucky one. I wish I was living in the States," he said. Since he is in the Haram, you know, I'm sure you've done like hundreds of *umrah* and ḥajj and he ended up saying that, *wallāhi*, he didn't do a single *ḥajj* or a single *umrah*. I said why not? He said it's too expensive. Too expensive to do what? *Umrah* doesn't cost you any money. You're just you're coming from the airport. You put the *iḥram* on, you say *labbayka 'umrah* and you just do *ṭawaf* and *sa'ie*. He said, "As a matter of fact, I never laid my eyes on the Ka'abah. I've never set a foot in the Haram, so I asked him why not how come you're 20 plus? I said my father never took me there. So, is the father blameworthy? Of course he is blameworthy. Well, he's not blameworthy for his son's disbelief. No. Why not? Because he did not spare an effort, it was his son who refused. When my children are born in Islam and I made certain to choose a good mother for them. They grew up seeing me and their mother praying, fasting, even voluntarily, fasting, sitting after *Fajr* reading Quran without saying much. They will follow us. A child who's only two years old. When Sarah, my daughter started crawling. She would grab her mother's hijab whenever it is a prayer time and she will spread the prayer rug and she will pray against the *qiblah*, you know, backward. But it's very lovely. I enjoy seeing that. And it's not only my Sarah. Every child is like that. Like mother, like daughter, like father, like son. So if you fell short and you do not do your job, you are blameworthy. I met this guy who was an engineer in the States. He's 30 plus. He doesn't know anything about the *deen*—even the prayers doesn't know how to read Qur'an, even though he was born and raised in Saudi. His parents are not Arab. They were expats living there. So I was wondering, he said he lived all his life in Saudi. Because his parents were working there. I said, isn't it weird that you don't even know how to read Qur'an? You don't speak Arabic, he said. Well, I know an Arabic word. One word for 30 years. From birth until you were thirty, you only knew one Arabic word he said. Yes, obviously you're all interested to know what is the word? Aren't you? Yeah, he said *shisha*. *Wallāhi*. So of course the parents are blameworthy. They didn't do their job and they also lost. It is a requirement to teach your children how to pray, how to fast. And it is a requirement for the mother. The girl now is only 8-9, ten years old. She keeps an eye on her. She started observing that she's reaching puberty. She's got to prepare her mentally. There's something called the menses. The period likewise. But the boy is, I've got to tell them there's something called wet dreams. And whenever you experience that, don't worry about it. This is a sign of reaching puberty. And it would be required that you should perform *ghusl*. If you didn't tell them, how would they know he's now 25 and he's been experiencing wet dreams and never done *ghusl* in his life? Why? Because he didn't know. No one had told him.